A WOMAN ENTREPRENEUR'S GUIDE
TO BUSINESS TRANSITION

POISED *FOR*

‹EXIT›

SECOND EDITION

JULIE KEYES

CERTIFIED EXIT PLANNER

INDIE BOOKS
INTERNATIONAL®

ISBN: 978-1-957651-02-6
Library of Congress Control Number: 2020907740

First edition designed by Joni McPherson
Second edition designed by Steve Plummer
Cover designed by Brittany Olson

First edition published 2020
Second edition published 2022

INDIE BOOKS INTERNATIONAL, INC®
2424 VISTA WAY, SUITE 316
OCEANSIDE, CA 92054
www.indiebooksintl.com

Praise for *Poised For Exit*

"I have one word for this book—empowering. An entrepreneur, especially who is a woman, often wears all the hats…except the hat that ensures she takes care of herself, her financial security and her legacy. Julie provides not only the inspiration and the promise of exiting gracefully and strongly, but she also provides the roadmap to make it happen. Don't pass up the opportunity to take control over your future—read the book and follow her advice. You only have one shot at this."

ERIN TURNER, ATTORNEY/CO-FOUNDER, JOHNSON TURNER LEGAL

"Julie's lived it. She's spent most of her career as a business owner and knows what keeps them up at night. It was a blessing to our community that she exited her business to start KeyeStrategies, launch the Twin Cities Exit Planning Institute Chapter and impart her wisdom locally and across the country. She's a go-to on successful exits and Poised for Exit, *is just another gift she's given us."*

JON KEIMIG, DIRECTOR, UNIVERSITY OF ST. THOMAS FAMILY BUSINESS CENTER

"Men and women approach running their businesses differently and they also think about exiting differently. Having sold three of my own businesses, everything Julie shares is so true. Every female business entrepreneur should take the time to read this quick and engaging book that highlights the importance of planning for an exit. Afterall, we plan everything else, so let's plan this most important event!"

LINDA ROSE, FOUNDER AND PRESIDENT OF ROSE BIZ. AUTHOR OF *GET ACQUIRED FOR MILLIONS*

"In your hands you hold a blueprint for creating value in your business. Julie shares what you need to know and what you need to do to define success on your terms and to see success in your succession. You have worked too hard to get where you are and deserve the financial and intangible rewards of your work effort."

MARK LEBLANC, CSP, AUTHOR OF *NEVER BE THE SAME* AND *GROWING YOUR BUSINESS!*

"Julie's book is filled with real-life stories and actionable tips. And even a few bonus cartoons. Keep in mind she can help you prepare as in her words, 'Your business exit will likely be the biggest financial transaction of your life, and for the majority, you have one shot at doing it right.'"

CATHY PAPER, M.A., PRESIDENT ROCK PAPER STAR

"The following book is a beautiful representation of how Julie approaches her work with clients. She first helps the owner define their objectives and goals, then assembles the team members to help the owner achieve those stated goals and objectives. Like Julie herself, this book is inspirational, authentic, and a guide to assist the female entrepreneur in achieving her goal of harvesting the wealth from her business."

Amy Wirtz, CEPA, J.D., Family and Business Success, LLC

"The stories shared in the book each had segments that could have been about my company, including treating employees like family, lower accountability for some members, and relatable obstacles. The positive perspective they were presented with was so encouraging, inspired me, and I'm now digging deeper for the grit I once had and to prepare for 'owner-readiness' in a more significant way.

I can honestly say, reading this book, at this time in my life, has changed my viewpoint on my exit strategy and I feel even more confident with who I am selecting to walk through the journey with, shoulder to shoulder. Together we are stronger, thank you, Julie for writing this book, and for making a positive impact on my future."

Marnie Ochs-Raleigh, CEO, Evolve Systems, Past President, NAWBO MN

"Julie Keyes knows what she's talking about when it comes to strategic, long-term thinking about business, business succession planning, what it means to plan for and exit a business, and the implications on life after exiting a business. I've had the pleasure of knowing Julie and working with her at a mutual client for the past several years. The creative thinking and valuable insights she has brought to this family owned company have helped them navigate through several important challenges and emerge stronger as a company. When Julie told me about this book, I thought, who better to write a book about business transition for women business owners? After reading the book my reaction is the stories, lessons, and advice she shares from her strong experience base are powerful and inspiring, both from what and how to do things as well as what not to do. Julie's stellar reputation in the local business community as well as her leadership in the field of business transition planning and execution make her uniquely qualified to write this book and we are all the beneficiaries. Great work and thank you Julie."

KEN SADDLER, MBA, PARTNER, CERTIFIED BUSINESS TRANSITION EXPERT™, B2B CFO®

"*In* Poised for Exit, *Julie Keyes uses her personal and professional experience to reach out to the ever-growing numbers of entrepreneurial women who, alone or with their spouses and family, have built successful enterprises and are now looking at 'what's next?' That experience allows Julie to tap into unique perspectives of female entrepreneurs.* Poised for Exit *uses real life situations and checklists to guide readers toward the type of personal, financial and business preparedness that will be critical to their successful transitions. Julie writes with the passion and sincerity that characterizes her devoted service to clients.*"

J. CHRISTOPHER CUNEO, ATTORNEY, BALLARD SPAHR, LLP

"*Julie Keyes' book* Poised for Exit *provides great advice for women in all stages of their business owner journey, whether they are looking to exit soon or thinking about how to plan for an exit in the future. Replete with stories and examples, Julie's book is a road map to help women through growing, scaling, and exiting a business and then deciding what's next. It is a book women will want to read again and again, underlining its pages and coming back to its wisdom, as they consider each step in the trajectory of their businesses and their lives.*"

TERRI KRIVOSHA, MERGERSA AND ACQUISITIONS ATTORNEY, PARTNER, MASLON LLP

"This book is an essential read for not only women entrepreneurs but anyone who owns a business. Julie presents the exit planning process in simple terminology and provides real life examples of what business owners could and will face. Julie provides you with a thoughtful framework of where to start and what entrepreneurs need to consider for a successful and profitable exit. Even if you're years away from retirement, it's never too early to think about how you want to leave your legacy!"

MAUREEN MAHONEY, CLIENT ENGAGEMENT SPECIALIST, HOOPIS PROFESSIONAL NETWORK

Contents

by Nicki Vincent, CAE

As a woman business owner, entrepreneur, real estate broker and association executive who drives growth in the middle market, I see first-hand how business owners can become paralyzed over the process of preparing their companies for sale. Sometimes the paralysis can be so real the sale never materializes because the owners often get in their own way. There are so many steps to prepare for a sale that details can be missed and viable options overlooked. Many business owners don't know where to turn, so they choose to do nothing.

What I have learned over the years in dealing with owners, operators, private equity, ESOPs, carveouts, and mergers and acquisitions in general is that many business owners simply don't know or speak the language, thus they and their companies are ill-prepared at the time of sale. Business owners know that succession planning is critical, yet upwards of 75 percent have no written transition plan in place. They are and have been heads down in the business for years, working hard and making it what it is. Many do so because they are passionate about what they do; they created something greater than themselves. Over time, the passion they once had can fade, yet they find themselves still working because their companies are not transferable. Whatever the situation, a business transition is usually very difficult to navigate, especially if the owner doesn't have the right team of advisers in place. The sale of a business is probably the largest financial transaction an owner will ever make, yet it can fall apart at the seams without the proper advice. Understanding the scope and scale of preparing an owner and their business for transition, as well as conveying the options, requires expertise from people who work in the field and do it every day. A Certified Exit Planner, like Julie Keyes, understands how to help the owner position their company to achieve an optimal outcome. Owners can set their company up for a successful transition by implementing effective processes and systems, securing key talent, and diversifying their customer base—to name a few options.

It's important to remember that one day, you will be gone from the business. How you leave your legacy is up to you. Whether you leave it to your family, your employees, or sell to a private equity group or strategic buyer, you need to first clarify your personal needs and wants. Trusted advisers are the key to exiting on your terms and not leaving money on the table. My friend and colleague Julie Keyes is herself a business owner and has been an entrepreneur for over thirty years. This experience truly gives her an edge as a consultant, as her clients go through this process of navigating the sale of their businesses, because she has been there herself and has lived through what keeps owners up at night.

When you are selling something of great value, like a business, you usually have one chance to do it right; thus the risk of doing it poorly is extremely high. Trusted advisers, therefore, are worth their weight in gold. Think of the sacrifices you've made to build your empire. Don't squander the opportunity for a future successful sale by not preparing.

Throughout this entire book, Julie will walk you through how to begin the process of preparing for your future exit. The advice is spot-on and delivered in a very simple, yet comprehensive, manner. Julie's expertise is only matched by her myriad connections to advisers in other disciplines, which give her an edge in helping owners vs. her ability to help an owner form a good team. It's one of her most sought-after professional attributes. As you will see in the appendix, Julie has assembled wisdom from some of the most prominent professional services firms in the country, insuring you'll have the very best advice to get you started. Use this book as a tool to do just that. Assemble your team of advisers and secure your financial future.

Not only does she run one of the most successful chapters in the country for the Association for Corporate Growth (ACG), Nicki Vincent is also the owner and Broker of Dona Properties, a boutique real estate firm specializing in residential, commercial, and business brokering. In addition to her work nationally and locally, she and her husband also own Action Fireworks and Kites, in both Wisconsin and Minnesota, so she's no stranger to entrepreneurism. Nicki has over twenty years' experience as the Executive Director of ACGMN, a global networking organization. Through this role Nicki, has become a master connector and drives growth in the middle and emerging markets through these relationships.

Preface

There are roughly 11 million baby boomers who currently own small businesses in the United States. Yet, the "tsunami" of exits has yet to occur. One reason has to do with the concept of "readiness." This book is meant to help prepare you and your firm for an exit based on your own terms. The stories told are of real clients, whose names and certain identifying details have been changed to protect confidentiality and anonymity.

Regardless of your age, gender, industry, or company size, you will eventually need to exit from your business. How well you exit is largely dependent upon how well and early you plan. Your business exit will likely be the biggest financial transaction of your life, and for the majority, you have one shot at doing it right. The tools and checklists in this book are meant to help you lay some of the groundwork. Let your advisers do the heavy lifting.

Thank you for taking the time to read this book. My hope and prayer is you achieve the best possible outcome for your future exit.

Be well,

Julie

How Many Chances Do You Have?

What is it about the prospect of being an entrepreneur that wired you to take more risk than a normal person? Where did that fire within come from to start and run your own business? Do you remember how you felt in those early days? Is it different from the way you feel now about your business? Let's explore these questions as we start to unwrap the process of transition planning. It's important to look back on where you've been before you choose your transition path for the future, if for no other reason than to pat yourself on the back for staying with the struggle!

When Deb bought her business from the founder in 1998, she was ecstatic about becoming a business owner. After the closing, she started finding issue after issue with the business and the honeymoon ended. From learning of antiquated software systems that didn't interface, to an inaccurate inventory report, to the sudden termination of a key person, she had her hands full right out of the gate. The former owner was long gone, and she was left to clean up a mess. Unfortunately, none of these matters came up in due diligence, or she could have had help finding a remedy before signing on the dotted line.

Over a period of ten years, Deb did the best she could on her own to improve operations and profitability but being, as the saying goes, the chief cook and bottle washer, made it tough for her to wear all the hats well. When we met, sales were flat, and she was quickly losing the desire for growing her empire. We put a growth and improvement plan together and after a couple of years, operations and profits were humming along better than ever. Sales were up due to a rock star-like new hire and Deb had more time to think and plan. That's when we started talking about a timeline for exit. It took us three years, but we grew her lifestyle business into an asset she could sell and sell she did. She now lives near the sunny beaches of the Gulf Coast and is living a life she only dreamed could come true.

Here's a story that didn't end as well and illustrates how a company's demise can be tied back to something as simple and preventable as the owner's personal stubbornness. Lois founded and operated a small business for over twenty years before we met. Her business never grew because she had a hard time giving up control of every detail. Her philosophy: delegation was for people who had a team they could trust, yet she lacked what it took to revive or replace the underperforming team members she'd hired and for whatever reason chose to retain. She knew she needed outside help to find the right people, but was afraid to make the investment, so she attempted to grow and manage her business without competent help. Her inability to delegate finds her in basically the same spot after twenty-seven years: still trying to do it all herself and still can't turn a decent profit and all the while trying to save her team from their habitual underperformance. Her business is so dependent upon her, that if she left for more than two weeks, it would suffer severely. If she were absent for more than a month, she'd be looking at a fire sale. All those years of decisions made without the help of competent advisers resulted in Lois owning a job rather than an asset. At sixty-six, she's stuck and must keep working to support her lifestyle. A sad story, yet it was preventable.

You may be one of the many woman business owners who fears the inevitable, bittersweet day that you will have to exit from your business. You may be asking yourself, "Who am I without my business?" or "What will become of my employees?" or "Who could run this business better than I can?" If any of those questions resonate with you, you're not alone. On the flip side, you may also be wondering how the process of exit planning works. Who's involved and when should you start planning and implementing your own exit strategy? You may even be asking yourself what life after business will be like, or *is* there life after business?

This book is intended to raise the consciousness of women who own and run their own companies but are unclear what a successful exit entails, who's involved, and what exit options might be available to them.

Let's face it: the likelihood of you finding a buyer or successor who would or could run the company just as you have is impossible. Why? Because we're all different. That doesn't mean that the company culture, brand, and market focus would necessarily change; but the way any person leads and grows a business and manages its employees varies. That realization can be tough to wrap your arms around. (You may even be afraid of being bested; if you are, you're not alone.)

If I know you as well as I know other female entrepreneurs (myself included), you do it all, and most often at a dead-run: you run a successful company, you run the kids, run the household, run to Target, run to the gym or the salon; but one thing you may not be good at is stillness. How could you be when you're always on task? Becoming a human being, as opposed to a human doing, will be an adjustment. Some of you are still raising kids, trying to build a marriage, and volunteering to boot. As born leaders both on and off the field, leading is something you naturally do; but leadership can be exhausting, especially if you have a hard time saying "no." This book is meant to help you stop the madness and breathe, and to take the time you need to think through the process of exit planning. In order to reach the light at the end of the tunnel, you need a guide. Someone who can walk the journey with you that is typically longer and more complicated than you think; you don't want to go it alone.

Jen owned a reputable commercial construction company—not an industry where you find many women. She learned most of what she knew about her industry and running a business the hard way, so she learned to make changes with great caution. Her employees were some of the most loyal I'd ever met, and she returned their loyalty with the same amount or even more. She worked long hours for many years because delegation did not come easy to her. When I became her adviser, one of my earliest recommendations was to replace two of her four department managers, because after working with them myself to try and redeem their performance, I determined they weren't a strong fit and did not align with the company values. It was doing neither they nor the company's core values any good to retain them and Jen knew she needed to find replacements, but terminations came hard for her. She had become like an office mother to many of her staff and they treated her as such. She was more of a confidante than a boss in some ways. Unfortunately, she had to learn the downside to playing a maternal role in her own company the hard way several times over before she finally stopped giving so many second chances. Yet, aside from all this confusion about her roles, her hard work and reputation within the industry truly preceded her, and she was still the owner of a successful, woman-owned construction company. Over the years, she and her company won many awards for industry leadership and innovation and gained a strong reputation as a great company to work for.

As we worked together, Jen allowed me to introduce other advisers who helped her plan a future transition from the business. The first was a financial adviser. Jen and her husband, who also owned a business, had holdings and investments in several places, so they needed an advisory firm who could help them organize their financial house as well as help them plan for their future. Andy, the financial adviser, did a great job of explaining things so the average person could understand their options. He also helped Jen get her corporate assets organized and created a corporate investment account as a method for key employee retention. In addition, he worked on a long-term plan with future income projections, so she and her husband would know how and whether they could maintain their current lifestyle after they exited their companies. Once her finances were organized with plans in place for her business and her personal life, Jen said she felt a great burden lifted as her fear of financial unknowns went away.

Jen and I then met with a couple of attorneys: one to help draft employee retention agreements and to update the company's maintenance contracts with key customers and another to update her family estate plan. With her legal and financial houses in order, we moved on to obtain a baseline valuation of the business from her accounting firm. In order for her financial house to be in complete order, she needed to know the value of her company, so as to determine whether a gap existed between the company's worth and what her financial adviser deemed she and her husband needed to maintain their current lifestyle.

Jen now feels like she's got more control over her own destiny and that feeling of security helps her sleep at night. Her company is running well, integrated systems are in place, and she has the right people in the right leadership seats. With her personal financial plan dialed in, she's ready for an exit whenever the time is right. She currently has a few options for this and is determining if she wants to pursue an internal sale like a management buyout with some key people who have expressed a strong interest or to entertain offers from the external solicitors who keep calling to see if she's ready to sell. She's still got a few years left at the helm, but the best part is that she's got options she didn't have before and she understands them. When she's ready to take her shot at exit, she'll likely hit a bullseye, because both she and her business are prepared. Jen's decided that once she retires she's going to freelance as a volunteer adviser for her industry, sit on a few Boards, and spend a lot more time at the family lake house with her grandkids.

CHAPTER 1 **CHECKLIST**

☐ Make a list of all the things you'd love to do but don't have the time.

☐ Prioritize the above.

☐ Begin looking at your company as if you were the buyer; would you buy it? If not, why not?

☐ Engage in, plan, and implement one of the items you listed in #2 and #3.

☐ Check out the tool in the Appendix from Sunbelt Business Advisers on how to build enterprise value on P. 110

☐ Do some journaling: Identify and write about the differences in how you feel about your business right now versus how you felt when you first launched.

CHAPTER 1
QUOTES BY FAMOUS WOMEN

*"I never dreamed about success,
I worked for it."*

—ESTÉE LAUDER

*"We need to accept that
we won't always make the
right decisions, that we'll
screw up royally sometimes—
understanding that failure is not
the opposite of success, it's part
of success."*

—ARIANNA HUFFINGTON

*"I have learned over the years
that when one's mind is made up,
this diminishes fear; knowing
what must be done does away
with fear."*

—ROSA PARKS

STATISTIC

"As of 2017, more than 11.6 million firms are owned by women in the United States, which generate over $1.7 trillion in annual sales." *The 2017 State of Women-Owned Businesses Report*

Ventureneer with the support of CoreWoman, commissioned by American Express, *The 2017 State of Women-Owned Businesses Report*, n.d., https://about.americanexpress.com/sites/amer-icanexpress.newshq.businesswire.com/files/doc_library/file/2017_SWOB_Report_-FINAL.pdf

©Glasbergen
glasbergen.com

"There will be six designated yawning breaks during my presentation. Please pace your boredom accordingly."

Chapter 2

How Do You Choose The Right Advisers?

Do you cringe when you look through the mail and see a hefty bill from one of your professional advisers? Paying fees for professional services can be painful (even for me, and I'm an adviser myself!); however, attempting to save a dime can cause you to spend a dollar by not getting proper, competent advice. I've learned my own valuable lessons when it comes to choosing a competent adviser: one who's worth their salt is worth every cent. While it's important to vet advisers for fit, reputation, and expertise, once you find one, retention is the next step—not saying "I'll think about it" and then attempting to do it yourself. Fee shock is normal, but obtaining sound, competent advice will not only speed up the exit-planning process for you, and save you thousands in self-made mistakes and wasted time, but can actually increase the multiple of what you will get for your business, along with what you get to *keep* after Uncle Sam gets his share. Here's a story that underlines the importance of choosing advisers with the proper expertise.

Lisa and her husband Tim decided it was time to sell their company after many years of toil, sacrifice, and sporadic adversity. Like many other entrepreneurs, they paid their dues the hard way and wanted out. They had no family members interested in taking over, so they had to sell to an outside third party. They assumed by working with me, they could accomplish a sale in a short time without much additional help. Even though they'd learned, through my guidance, that it would take a team of advisers to help orchestrate a successful exit, they decided they'd do the bulk of the exit work on their own. I had introduced them to some competent people in the exit-planning space: to start with, an accountant and an attorney who each specialized in mergers and acquisitions. But Lisa and Tim decided these advisers' fees were too high and opted to retain neither of them, even though they could well afford the best in class. They chose instead to use their company's long-time litigation lawyer, who knew little about mergers and acquisitions law; in addition, they relied on their accountant, who had been with them since the company's inception, but who did not offer valuation services and was not a CPA. Both of these advisers were well intentioned, intelligent professionals, but neither was schooled in exit planning.

They put the company on the market with an investment banker and received several good offers for the business, but in the end sold it internally to their management team and for half of what they could have gotten from an external buyer; that's how badly they wanted out. During this process, they kept me out of the loop, because they knew I would try to save them from themselves, and went ahead with a closing. They received almost no cash up front and held a Note Payable for nearly the entire balance. They also agreed to an imbalanced earn-out due to the lack of legal expertise they received. Now, they are committed to working many more years than they had planned in order to collect what's owed them on the sale of their business, the assets of which they still need to retire. As a result of not wanting to pay fees for competent advice, they can't take their eye off the ball as they had hoped and dreamed. The lack of professional advice they received severely compromised their own financial security, yet saved them a few thousand dollars in fees. How's that for a fair trade?

Now that you've heard about what not to do, let's contrast Lisa and Tim's story with the experience of owners who made good choices. John and Marion owned and operated their business for thirty-two years. John began the journey out of his garage and Marion soon joined him. They made quite a team; however, they lacked the capital they needed for their business to grow quickly. As a result, it took them a long time to build their business into a transferrable asset, but they did it. They suffered through many tough times, such as when they couldn't pay themselves, lost key clients, made poor hiring decisions, and had reluctance to delegate (any of these resonate with you?). When I first met with John and Marion, they had been toying with the idea of selling. With no internal successor, they started focusing on an external sale to a third party. We began our work with a plan to de-risk them financially, legally, and personally, with the help of their other professional advisors and then moved on to prepare their business for transition.

Soon after I began to work with them, John and Marion received a call from a national competitor in pursuit of so-called industry consolidation, who wondered if my clients might be interested in selling. This call prompted an accelerated exit-planning project, because the caller was not just any competitor, but one of the few competitors they'd actually considered selling to. Thankfully, John and Marion had built a desirable, transferable entity and had already done some essential work in preparing themselves and their business for transition, so they were ahead of the game. It turned out that the competitor sent us a Letter of Intent within two weeks of the initial call. The due diligence period covered less than ninety days and the closing occurred without a glitch. They received an offer from a cash buyer with no earn out!

That's what you call an ideal situation and all because John and Marion prepared as much as they could ahead of time. One essential thing they did was to assemble a very strong team of advisers. They also spent time thinking about when they wanted to be completely out of their business and what they would do afterward. John and Marion are planning their first two-week vacation ever to visit their homeland of the Netherlands. After some fun travel plans, John plans to start an industry consulting business and Marion plans to babysit her grandchildren more. Life is good for John and Marion. They got more for their business than they thought they'd get because they had outside expertise to help them navigate a beneficial outcome. They also did a good job of diversifying their client base, building their brand, delegating to competent key personnel, and keeping profits a front-and-center, lifelong priority.

My entrepreneurial journey started in 1989, and for twenty years, my husband and I started and grew four separate companies in three locations. We provided various legal- and title-related services to realtors and builders in both residential and commercial real estate transactions. We built a great reputation as a non-affiliated, independent firm, and over time we experienced much success. Even though 90 percent of our competition involved real estate firms with their own in-house title and lending services who didn't necessarily need outside services, we still managed to get business from professionals who were more interested in providing their clients with expert advice and great service over receiving kickbacks from their in-house affiliations. Over the years, we rode many waves through various market conditions, usually faring better than our larger competitors during downturns. The advantage we had, was that we performed all of the services ourselves, including legal services and only used outside vendors for short-term projects or lower-end services. Being industry experts and nimble at the same time provided us a niche in a saturated industry, making it easier for me to sell a relationship with our firm, once they gave us a try. We won the long-term loyalty of many, because of our expertise, but also because we knew what made our clients tick and believed it was our job to make them look good.

We owned three separate companies and I held a dual role in business development and business management for all three of them. We had offices in four locations at one time and eventually merged two of them. Still with three locations, you can imagine how much running I did; it's a wonder I ever got anything done. You probably remember when dial-up was our only link to cyberspace; those were the days. When technology advanced, unfortunately it did not do so all at once in our market areas. We had to have a separate server in all three locations, and yet we thought it was the best thing ever compared to all the years of using fax machines for electronic communication. When we were first able to get online it was dial-up only, then a few years later we hit the big time; one office had DSL, one had a T-1 line and one was still dial-up. To say we had technology nightmares when attempting to share files would be an understatement. (Wi-Fi didn't become available until after we sold our companies.)

I think for me, the hardest part of being a business owner was in managing the employees. Some people are leaders and some are managers. I learned that I am much more the former over the latter. Had I been a better manager of people, I think I could have alleviated many of our staffing problems a lot sooner. My husband was not the management type either; he preferred to be left alone. His kind of ownership style didn't lend itself to building a great culture, so that was my job too. On the business development side, I handled all of the sales, marketing, advertising and trade association memberships. I knew our market and all the major players, and they all knew me. I got pretty good at seeking and vetting growth opportunities for the company; some turned out to be our best moves. Being a smaller company meant we could make changes much quicker than our competitors, but we also didn't have the resources they had when compliance requirements became mandated. In my mind, the best way to remedy that was to grow to be as big as we could. One of my strategies for growth was in opening on-site closing offices for the convenience of our realtor and builder clientele. Using this method I was able to negotiate and secure two lucrative strategic partnerships for our firm that not only tripled our annual revenue, but became sources of recurring sales. We became relevant to our competition at that point and having to "prove" myself to our industry became less of a preoccupation for me.

With all those responsibilities for me at the office, I often found myself wishing I could be home with my kids. I did my best to spend as much time with them as I could, especially when they were off of school, but they definitely had their share of time in the office on Saturday mornings waiting for me to get one more thing done. During the busiest times, they spent many hours playing "racecars" with the swivel office chairs, tic tac toe on the white boards, and drawing their own cartoon characters with felt-tip highlighters. Sometimes the drawings were made on important paperwork. That never went over well on Monday morning, for some reason. The boys were older, so they were "in charge" of the office chairs and the girls could only use them if they sat down and let the boys "drive." Tyler, my oldest, spun my daughter, Natalie, so many times the chair came off the base. Making for another not-so-happy employee on Monday morning, for sure.

We owned a lake cabin for many years in northern Minnesota to help us get away from the office and force ourselves to relax. Many times in the summer, we'd leave on Friday morning to beat the rush up north. It was one such Friday when I got a call I'll never forget. I was standing on the deck watching my kids jump off the dock when my cell phone rang. A man's gruff-sounding voice on the other end said, "I've got Shannon tied up in the trunk and I'm driving her to Mexico!" followed by maniacal laughter just before he hung up. "Shannon" was our newest hire. She hadn't been with us for more than a couple of weeks. We didn't know anything about her personal life, other than that she had a boyfriend. After I recovered from my initial shock I tried numerous times to dial back, but no answer. I then had to call the office and tell my office manager where I kept the key to my file cabinet so she could pull the HR file I had on Shannon and give me her next-of-kin phone numbers; none of whom would take my call or answer my messages. It seemed I was being duped, but how could I know for sure? As it turned out, Shannon's boyfriend was the caller. We learned this on Monday morning, when she flounced into the office for work, giggling about what a practical joker he was. A long weekend of worry on my part for nothing. Shannon didn't last much longer on the payroll. I tell this story because it is one of many such situations we find ourselves in as business owners. If you have had it happen, I've probably lived through it myself. I understand what you're going through and I have felt much of the same pain.

In 2007, my husband had an accident and couldn't work for over a year. As our attorney, he played an integral role on the production side of the business, so his absence was a real problem for us. In 2009 I was forced to sell the business assets, because my husband had not fully recovered and became despondent. To top it off, the main tenant in our office building took the opportunity to stop paying rent during this time, so after several months of his promises to catch up, I had to evict him. Evicting a tenant is not easily done in Minnesota and I had to hire legal counsel to do it. His hefty debt to us couldn't be collected because he subsequently committed suicide and we learned his estate was penniless.

Between 2007 and 2010, several more calamities became a perfect storm of adversity. After selling the business, I went back to my former career as a mortgage loan officer to pay the bills; an experience that confirmed I'm not cut out to work for someone else. I hated my job and became depressed. Two depressed people in the same house is too many and after so many years of heavy burdens and not enough love, our marriage crumbled. Getting divorced was the toughest thing I'd ever done in my life. It was something I never thought would happen to me.

The many life changes and losses all at once were stressful for all of us. I remember not sleeping much and maxing out my credit cards to support my two younger children who were still in school and heavily involved in sports, since my ex-husband paid only $100 per month in child support, which he achieved more through legal manipulation than economic hardship. My two older sons had moved out, but we remained close. To this day, they are my knights in many ways. After the divorce, I took another job with a larger bank and higher commission, so I could qualify to buy my own house. I wanted my daughters and I to have a better chance of building a new normal and living in an apartment didn't cut it. During this time of life transition, I knew I would one day start another business, but I didn't know what it would be. I had good support in my family and friends; I often asked them where they saw me making the most impact in the world. My mantra was that life was going to be better than ever and I would do life-changing work for a living; I just didn't know yet what that would be.

Three separate times over the course of a couple years, I was approached by unrelated people, to consider becoming a business coach or consultant. I politely declined the first two offers. When the third came along, I decided God was trying to tell me something and I listened more intently. Marti was the third person who suggested I become a business coach. She was a licensee of a national coaching franchise and she was convinced I was a perfect candidate for the work. However, I wasn't so sure I wanted to take the risk after just getting divorced and buying a house, so I dragged out the decision to try the coaching field for another six months.

During that time, I again made the rounds with my family and friends and specifically asked, "Should I do this work?" They unanimously said yes. So, I signed up to work for Marti as an independent consultant under her franchise license. I had been given the opportunity to buy my own license, but decided to wait and see what the company was like first before taking that risk. It was required that I travel to the East Coast for some intensive certification training. When I returned, I began the journey to build my practice. It turned out that Marti had been overly optimistic about how rapidly my practice would grow and that I'd have so many leads pouring in from the company, I'd need an assistant to keep up. The truth was that I received no leads from the company at all. Every client I acquired came from my own relentless effort. The franchisor she bought her license from was money-motivated and charged us high fees for ineffective, antiquated technology and unproductive lead generation methods. Even though I received major awards from them two years in a row for top performance, my commitment to rebuilding my future came first and I had to move on. When I first started consulting, Marti tried hard to be a good mentor. She admitted, "You know Julie, this work is not easy to do. In fact, most people are not cut out to do what we do for business owners. It's also difficult to build a process for your clients and keep your pipeline full at the same time, but I know you have what it takes to make it happen. You've got the perfect background to make a great adviser for business owners because you've lived through the challenges they're facing every day."

Over the next several years my business grew and I received great reviews and referrals. I found myself feeling grateful to have found my life's work.

As I became more known in professional circles, I was asked to do some speaking and presenting, especially around the topic of exit strategy. After conducting workshops and presentations on the subject for a couple of years, I learned about the Exit Planning Institute from a trusted colleague who had just been through the CEPA program. A few months later, in 2015, I became a Certified Exit Planning Adviser. Ever since then I've been on a mission to help as many business owners as possible plan and implement a graceful exit. I am especially drawn to woman business owners because, from what I've learned, there are no guides or books specifically written for women on how to exit gracefully. I've since expanded my efforts and gained exposure through teaching, speaking, and writing in order to reach a larger audience of business owners, so that I can make a positive impact in a shorter period. I had limited advisory when I sold my own business assets. It would have been great for me had I started the readiness process and established better advisory long before disaster, in the form of my then-husband's illness and the recession, struck.

Having right-fit advisers on your team is everything, so if you're not connected to whom you need, ask for referrals to trusted professionals from others who have worked with them. Be sure to meet with at least two potential advisers from each discipline before you retain anyone's services. You may need to meet with more than two advisers in order to determine a right fit. Just remember that fit is equally important to fee structure or proximity to the adviser's office!

CHAPTER 2 **CHECKLIST**

☐ List all of the advisers currently representing or previously representing you or your company.

☐ List the ones you want to retain. If you're letting anyone go, make sure they know about it, don't just ignore them. They may have documentation on file that you need in order to move on to the next adviser.

☐ Schedule a recurring semi-annual or quarterly group meeting with your advisers.

☐ Identify the gaps in advisory: who do you know that could give you a referral to a trusted adviser? (Estate or business lawyer, CPA, wealth manager, exit planner, banker, or insurance agent)

☐ What kind of traits would you expect from a trusted adviser? Do your current advisers match this list of traits?

☐ Ideally, what would you like your advisers to do for you? Do your current advisers know your wishes?

☐ Review the tools and checklists from the advisory firms highlighted in the Appendix.

CHAPTER 2
QUOTES BY FAMOUS WOMEN

"The difference between successful people and others is how long they spend time feeling sorry for the themselves."

—BARBARA CORCORAN

"I am not afraid of storms, for I am learning how to sail my ship."

—LOUISA MAY ALCOTT

STATISTIC

There are approximately 5.4 million firms are majority-owned by women of color in United States, according to The 2017 State of Women-Owned Businesses Report

Ventureneer with the support of CoreWoman, commissioned by American Express, *The 2017 State of Women-Owned Businesses Report*, n.d., https://about.americanexpress.com/sites/americanexpress.newshq.businesswire.com/files/doc_library/file/2017_SWOB_Report_-FINAL.pdf

"The local business journal wants to do an article on the 10 most powerful women in our company. Quick, go hire 7 more women!"

What Does It Mean For An Owner To Be Exit-Ready?

Janet wanted to spend more time on her hobby farm, but she was still engaged with her business full time. Here she was in her mid-sixties, a cancer survivor, and still burning the candle at both ends. When we met, she confided that she wasn't sure about whether anyone on her team was qualified to become her successor. After I met with each of her team members, I wholeheartedly agreed. After we discussed her dilemma in detail, Janet said, "Julie, what do you think I should do? I'm not a good manager of people. I'm more of a leader." I agreed with her self-assessment. Not everyone is a good manager, but many times people are made to be managers. Did you get into business just so you could manage people? I've never met an owner who answered yes to that question. However, as it goes with managing people, not everyone is a born leader, either. Janet hired the wrong people and put them in the wrong seats. It was after realizing this problem and understanding that her timeline for exit was looming, that she contacted me.

Janet had hired people who were not self-starters and who wouldn't make a move without her nod, thus tying her down even more to managing her managers. Yet her belief and optimism in her team was one of Janet's most endearing qualities and equally one of her most blatant faults. She had a hard time terminating her employees, as many owners do, and thus gave her team-members numerous second chances. (I've seen this pattern among other women who run companies; perhaps it's the "mother" in us.)

Unfortunately, she had used most of her personal assets to get the company back in the black after her recovery from cancer, so she needed to sell her business in order to move on to her next act—her hobby farm. As we worked together, we replaced most of her management team one by one. We then brought on an equity partner, who was hired to become her CEO. Approximately five years later, the company was highly profitable again and growing faster than ever. Janet still works in the business as a part-time consultant to her new partner, who is incrementally buying out her interest. It took her a lot longer to get her business ready for transition and she knew many of her obstacles were due to her own decisions, but she was finally able to step away from the business she worked so hard to build twice over.

Now she spends most of her waking hours as a hobby farmer and loves her hard-won freedom.

If you're like most owners, you're finding it difficult to imagine life without your business. How will you remain productive? How do you maintain a sense of fulfillment? If you decide to retire, are you certain you can maintain your current lifestyle? What about being psychologically and emotionally ready? If these questions are popping up for you, you're not alone. They're the most common concerns that owners face as they begin the process of exit and we're going to address them a bit in this chapter.

For women, it's especially difficult making the decision to exit. Why? Because women tend to put others' needs before their own, so planning a successful exit goes against how women are wired as nurturing people. As a woman business owner, you may have deep concerns over the welfare of your staff after you leave. You may also be worried about the financial pressure of making the leap to sell your company. It will probably be the biggest financial transaction of your life and you basically have one shot at doing it right. No pressure there! Couple that pressure with a woman's tendency to second-guess herself or put others' needs before her own, and you've got the recipe for why women tend to hesitate in planning their business exit.

Other aspects of being owner-ready means determining what the current value of your company is and identifying potential buyers or internal successors. Most owners have a number in their heads of what they think the business is worth and most of the time it's much higher number than what the market will actually bear; that's why you need to seek competent help in determining an accurate number now.

Similarly, the sooner you know whether you have internal successor candidates or not, the sooner you can prepare yourself and your company for that type of exit. There are many differences between an internal and an external sale. The checklists and tools in the back of the book will help get you started in the process of thinking this through.

You also need to mitigate any legal risk you may or may not know about. You can determine if your business faces any such risks by hiring a good business attorney who can conduct a legal audit for you. If there's one person you want on your side, it's a good attorney. Yes, they cost money, but let's consider what you could lose if you had no legal advice. Do you have any idea how much could you lose then? There's no way to calculate your potential loss. For example, if you have business partners, do you have a Buy Sell or Share Holder Agreement? When did you last update it? Do you have Key Person Insurance and Employment Agreements? Is your Estate Plan in place and if so, does it address the business? What about Contingency Planning?

You might be thinking, "Good grief, this process is going to be complicated and time-consuming." It can be, and usually is, which is why you need a strong team of advisers to help you along the way.

If there's one thing commonly overlooked in Exit Planning, it's Life Planning or Next Act Planning for the owners. Life after business is not all about fun and games. Let's face it: you've been working your tail off for how many years, and you think you can stop that all together and play 24/7? Even if you could afford to do that for the rest of your life, you will probably become bored and feel unproductive. If you're like most other owners, you have an ingrained desire for accomplishment; think of all you've learned and achieved. How can you harness that energy into something that's significant for you, but still allows you the freedom you want and deserve for checking off some bucket list items? Incidentally, if you don't have a bucket list, perhaps you start one now.

CHAPTER 3 **CHECKLIST**

☐ Contingency Plan (this is not an Estate Plan or in place of one).

☐ Discuss a baseline value of your company with your CPA firm.

☐ Normalize and maintain high quality financials going forward.

☐ Meet with your insurance agencies and get an audit of all your policies.

☐ Meet with your wealth adviser or financial planner about succession planning.

☐ Meet with your business attorney about legal risk mitigation for you and your business.

☐ Checkout my Transition Planning Checklist in the Appendix.

CHAPTER 3
QUOTES BY FAMOUS WOMEN

"A woman is like a teabag . . . only in hot water do you realize how strong she is. "

—ELEANOR ROOSEVELT

STATISTIC

"Between 1997 and 2017, the number of women-owned businesses increased by 114%, compared to a 44% increase among all businesses—a growth rate more than 2.5 times the national average."

The 2017 State of Women-Owned Businesses Report

Ventureneer with the support of CoreWoman, commissioned by American Express, *The 2017 State of Women-Owned Businesses Report*, n.d., https://about.americanexpress.com/sites/americanexpress.newshq.businesswire.com/files/doc_library/file/2017_SWOB_Report_-FINAL.pdf

Is Your Business Prepared For Anything?

Several years ago, I got a call from an attendee of a presentation I'd given two years prior (can you believe he kept my card that long?). He started the conversation like this:

"Hi Julie Keyes, this is Joe Smith. I attended a seminar of yours a couple years ago. Are you still doing exit-planning work?"

"Yes I am, Joe. I'm glad you kept my card. Tell me what your timeline for exit is and how you think I could help."

"Well, my wife Shelly and I talked and decided it's time for me to get out, so I'd like to get this done by the end of the year"—it was October—"so we should probably meet and get started, I suppose."

"OK," I said, "let's get together and talk about what we need to do," knowing full well we needed a lot more time than two months to do the exit right. It took us two years, but we got him out.

The reason the exit process took two years was because Joe's company needed several operational updates in preparation for a buyer. He had no internal successor, so selling externally was the best solution for him to achieve his retirement goal. Had he chosen to do nothing to prepare his business, he would have been eventually forced to shut it down or to sell some of the assets for pennies on the dollar, especially if his health continued to deteriorate. Losing his business asset would have eliminated his primary source of retirement and thus, would have negated all those years of risk, hard work, and sacrifice. This case is too often repeated by owners who have their retirement nest eggs tied up in their businesses. When a business lacks transferability, the equity an owner perceives to exist actually doesn't exist. We call this outcome the rude awakening; one that many owners have faced and many more will face in the coming years, due to a wide-spread lack of preparedness in our country.

A frightening statistic derived from "The State of Owner Readiness Survey" reports conducted by the Exit Planning Institute in Cleveland, Ohio tells us that over 50 percent of all businesses will suffer from one of the five Ds: divorce, death, disagreement, disability, and disaster. Luckily, Joe got out before one of the five Ds came knocking. Countless business owners have suffered from one or more of the five Ds and could tell sad stories of dashed dreams, the end of which were almost always preventable. Joe's wife, Shelly, had been pushing him to sell, so they could travel and enjoy life more at their lake home. She knew his health was in question and worried the stress of ownership would take a higher toll on Joe than it already had. Shelly's exit from the business had already occurred, and she hoped her exit would inspire Joe to plan his own. She wanted the two of them to do the things they'd always talked about doing but couldn't because of the business. After Joe had his first heart attack, he slowed down but didn't take his exit seriously until two years later, when his doctor said he needed to destress as soon as possible; that's when he called me. The lesson here is that we are almost never warned before one of the five Ds occurs. It's always best to ready yourself and your business just in case, regardless of whether you're selling soon or ten years from now.

What I find to be one of the main value detractors in small business is owner dependency due to over control by the owner. Joe's business could only function without him for a couple of weeks or maybe a month. He couldn't leave for any longer than that, because he had all his management team reporting to him. We changed that by promoting one of his best leaders to general manager. Lesson: make your business run without you.

Another issue Joe had was that the customers liked to call him when they needed a favor; he was the main salesperson for the company and his customers loved him. He got the job done and service was his middle name. We needed to replace him as the face of the business with someone else, so we hired a woman to take that spot. She had the perfect set of skills and experience; it was like she was meant for the job. Joe still got calls from customers, but in his friendly conversations, he would invite and remind them that he was no longer the go-to person. Over a few months, he stopped getting so many calls, which gave him a feeling of relief and the guilt he'd feel over being away on a long weekend or vacation dissipated, because he knew his customers had someone to call who could solve issues and keep them satisfied.

Once Joe was able to step away more frequently, we assembled a sales team to handle the company's various product and service lines. We also divided their revenue into buckets by department, which made tracking profitability much easier and cleaner. In less than two years, Joe's business went from $18 million in topline revenue to $26 million in topline revenue and we increased profit margins by an average of 5 percent by cutting waste and streamlining processes.

With these two value detractors reversed into value enhancers, we moved on to the finance area. His controller was just that: controlling. No wonder she and Joe didn't get along well—they both wanted control. She had been with the company almost since its inception twenty-six years prior and no one knew the company as well as she did, or so she thought. To remedy this problem, I spent a lot of time with the general manager to understand their profit drivers. We analyzed their cost of doing business, how they derived their margins, what jobs were most and least profitable, and examined missed billing opportunities. The latter turned out to be a major culprit that the controller was ignoring. Once we discovered the areas needing improvement, we involved her in the process of creating ways to remedy the issues. She was glad to be part of the solution once we shared what the issues were. Let's just say the financials looked a lot better a few months after that.

When Joe finally signed over the company to the new owners, it was like a huge load was lifted from his shoulders. I'd never seen him and Shelly smile so broadly. It was a beautiful thing! They're now remodeling their lake home and spending lots of time with their grandchildren. They've taken two European trips since the closing, with more destinations on the horizon. Life is good for Joe and Shelly.

Preparing a business for sale is not an overnight or do-it-yourself endeavor. If you find yourself in a situation like the one Joe was in, you're not alone. Many owners face those same issues. The key is to pull your head out of the sand and take decisive action. Doing so with the help of a business mentor or consultant will speed things up and give you comfort in knowing you have someone at your side.

There are many other aspects of business readiness or lack thereof that can derail any effort to sell a company. I've touched on a few in this story. For more on value detractors and what you need to do to get your business ready, see the tools and checklists in the back of the book.

CHAPTER 4 **CHECKLIST**

☐ Determine whether you have a company too dependent on you and begin to delegate and shift authority.

☐ Examine your customers or clients list. Are there any who represent more than 20 percent of your business?

☐ Are you overly dependent on any vendor, supplier, or employee? What could happen if you lost any one of them?

☐ Retain your key employees—or someone else will.

☐ Sales and marketing: Is it well-planned or shooting from the hip?

☐ Profit margin check in: Is it time to raise prices? Where's the wasted money?

☐ Cash flow analysis from your accounting firm.

☐ Utilize your CPA's expertise to compile an annual budget and three-year forecast.

☐ A strong brand builds enterprise value. How strong is your brand? (Recognizable in the marketplace, with highly regarded reputation).

☐ Check out the tool in the Appendix from Dunlap Seeger.

CHAPTER 4
QUOTES BY FAMOUS WOMEN

"Don't be intimidated by what you don't know. That can be your greatest strength and ensure that you do things differently from everyone else."

—SARA BLAKELY, FOUNDER OF SPANX

"Do one thing every day that scares you."

—ELEANOR ROOSEVELT

STATISTIC

"79 percent of small business owners have no written transition plan." Survey Data from the Exit Planning Institute

Exit Planning Institute. "2017 State of Business Owner Readiness Survey for the Twin Cities Metro Area". *Exit Planning Institute*, 2017. https://exit-planning-institute.org/

©Glasbergen
glasbergen.com

"If I talk to you about life insurance,
I can write off this vacation
as a business expense."

Chapter 5

Do You Understand Your Exit Options?

Siblings Sheri and Bruce were second-generation owners of a business their uncle had started over forty years ago. They both had worked in the business since their college graduations and held several different positions over their time with the company. Sheri was nine years older than Bruce and had a shorter timeline to exit than Bruce had. Even though they had their differences, they were both committed to doing whatever they could to carry on the family legacy.

I remember when we first started working together, Sheri would proudly tell me how many calls she'd received that week asking if she was ready to sell:

"Julie, I think my business is a hot commodity in our market, or I wouldn't be getting so many calls. This has to be true, because they always say they have a buyer who's expressed interest."

"What do you say when they ask to meet with you?" I asked.

"I tell them I'm not interested at this time and hang up. I'm still holding out on the hope that my son will want to take over someday. Is that a dumb wish?"

"Not at all, Sheri." I replied. "Tell me about your son and why you think he'd make a good successor to run the company."

Sheri then proceeded to tell me about her son, Jared. Jared took a job with an engineering firm in Chicago after college and had been working there three years, when he approached his mom during a family holiday party asking her what the future might hold for him in the business. He said he had been thinking about whether the company might be a good fit for his skills and if the company could use his talents. He wondered if someday he could come back to work there. He had worked there during high school and then as a college intern, but after graduation, Sheri encouraged him to work elsewhere before deciding to come back into the family business, which he did do. Even though Sheri never wanted him to leave, she knew sending her son off to work for someone else would be the best way for Jared to become more self-aware and learn what he wanted to do. Sheri hoped that after a few years she'd know whether Jared was a candidate as successor and could make her exit timeline decisions then. She wanted to have Jared back, but knew it had to be when Jared felt ready.

Sheri and I had discussed a common pitfall of family business owners to employ family members just because they're family, yet who may not possess the talent, skills, or desire for the job. A sense of family bloodline entitlement can taint company culture, spreading dysfunctional behavior between family members and non-family members alike. Knowing all of this, Sheri made a wise choice in sending Jared elsewhere for a while; and Jared's double major in engineering and marketing made for a great combination that the company could utilize. He also had his mom's people skills and was, like Sheri, self-driven and hardworking.

After hearing her story about Jared, I said, "From what you've told me, it seems to me that grooming Jared as a possible successor makes sense. You know there's no guarantee that he's a 'right fit,' but you won't know unless you keep the conversation alive and implement some leadership assessments as well. At first glance, it looks like a worthwhile pursuit. Also, you need to know those other offers you're getting are almost never legitimate. Those callers represent competitors or investors, looking for desperate sellers who need a way out. They're trained to entice the owners by complimenting them and building false rapport, and then try to create a false sense of urgency to act now."

Sheri replied, "I suppose that's true, but I still think we have a good investment opportunity in this company for somebody, even if Jared decides it's not for him."

"Yes, you do, but we have work to do in order to make it a more turn-key operation. Whether you're going to transfer it to Jared or sell it to a third party, there's work to get it ready. Your future financial security depends on that."

Sheri looked down as she thought about what I said. She knew it was going to be a lot of work to ready herself and the company for an eventual transfer. She said, "I know, Julie; that's what I'm afraid of. It's going to take a lot of my time, isn't it? But I know it needs to happen, so I'm willing to do what it takes to get things into shape around here. My brother Bruce plans to maintain his current role in sales but doesn't want my job. He will be a big part of our growth and improvement plan, however."

"Yes, he will," I said. "It *will* take time, Sheri, but as I see it, we don't have a choice. You and Bruce don't want to leave money on the table by not properly preparing, so it will be worth the investment to prepare you and the company. You and Bruce will then have more exit options to choose from. If you two determine Jared's not a candidate, you can seek out another leader to take over and you can continue to own the business. Another option would be to sell part of the company to a private equity firm who could grow your enterprise value and you take a second bite of the apple later on. Selling to a strategic buyer or competitor is another option. All of those become more viable once we've done our work together in getting it ready. Jared could even be a part of those options with a minority equity stake."

"I like options," said Sheri. "Let me know how your conversation goes with Bruce. We don't talk much about what each of us wants when it's all said and done, so it will be important for us to have that conversation. I'm glad you're here to help us sort this out."

"Yes, Bruce and I are meeting on this topic next week," I said.

When I met with Bruce, his concerns mirrored Sheri's, yet his timeline for exit was different. He believed Jared had what it took to take over for Sheri, so he was on board with the plan to test the waters.

"I can't imagine my life without working in this business," he said. "My mom raised us while working in this business; it's all I've ever known."

"I realize that, Bruce," I replied, "and I understand you're feeling apprehensive. I'm here to help you sort all of that out and determine what your future role here might look like. I'd like to see you taking more time off from the business by delegating to some of your support staff on a regular basis. It's important that you practice your eventual exit."

Bruce smiled and said, "Wouldn't it be great if I could work thirty hours a week instead of fifty-five or sixty? What a dream that would be! My wife and kids wouldn't know what to do with me, I'd have so much free time."

As it turned out, Jared decided to take the job offer from the family business and is currently being groomed to succeed his mom over the next five to seven years. Bruce plans to stay on for another ten years and the business is continually growing and making improvements to ensure a smooth transition and competitive position in the marketplace for years to come. In the meantime, they have hired a general manager to take on more of the day-to-day operational duties, so they can both begin to practice their exit by taking more time off.

Wayne and Mary Lou started a business right out of college. Wayne wanted to pursue his love of acting and with a degree in theatre, he began creating entertainment programs for corporate events. Word got out in the event planning industry that Wayne's programs were big crowd-pleasers and the company started to take off. Mary Lou's degree was in business administration, so as the other half of the business, she spent her time managing the finances and running the business operations. They made a great pair. Once they had a good number of steady clients, they decided it was time to move out of their basement and into a real office space. Over a period of twenty-six years, they built a successful business together, taking it from nothing to a best-in-class operation, generating several million in sales and growing every year. It wasn't always easy, but they managed to find a new normal and keep growing with each turn life took.

A few years ago, after losing their biggest client, they had a heart-to-heart discussion and realized they needed some outside help to make some big decisions about the future; it was all getting to be overwhelming without proper advisory. When we met, they were contemplating whether to sell the business to a third party or try to groom their son to take over. They wanted me to help assess their readiness as well as whether their son was the right candidate. After a couple of years and a lot of open and honest communication, we concurred that their son, Trey, would be their successor. Wayne and Mary Lou are still actively engaged in the business, but are practicing their future exit by leaving for a month at a time and delegating all decisions to Trey and their operations manager, Patti. They've got three years left before they begin their travel plans around the world and couldn't be more excited.

What are your options if you want to sell internally, but don't have family to sell to? Management buy-out is another option as well as an employee stock ownership plan (ESOP), if it makes sense for your company. ESOPs are generally best suited for companies with higher-salaried employees and lower debt service, such as professional services firms. Architectural firms and engineering firms tend to be good candidates for ESOPs, but recently other industries have jumped on board with ESOPs as well, such as manufacturing and distribution firms. ESOPs can be expensive to start and maintain but can also be a great way for owners to retain high-level employees, leave a legacy, and defer or eliminate capital gains on the sale of the business. If you want to learn more, discuss your questions with an ESOP specialist.

When an internal transfer is not an option, then it's time to seek out introductions to business brokers and investment bankers who can help you sell your business to a third party. You could sell all or part of your business. Investment bankers (those who sell companies with revenue of $10 million or more) tend to have relationships with private equity firms who seek to place their investment dollars in companies with strong profit margins and exceptional growth potential. If you'd like to infuse additional capital into your business, but stay on for a while, then private equity might be the answer. Smaller companies (those under $10 million in revenue) don't tend to be good prospects for private equity, but sometimes an investment banker can find a family office with interests in smaller businesses. If you're clear on your exit timeline, then putting it on the market right away might be the answer.

Jerry and Kate were so excited to pass the baton to their general manager, Aaron, whom they'd been grooming to succeed them. When I first met them to help them ready themselves for exit, they asked me to meet with Aaron on the side. Aaron confided in me that he wasn't sure anymore if he wanted to buy the company and he was afraid to tell Jerry and Kate. We talked about risk tolerance, financing, and the legal steps necessary to put the deal together. After all that discussion, Aaron concluded that he had to step aside. He was too afraid to take the risk of borrowing the money to buy the business from the owners, but he wanted to stay engaged as general manager. Jerry and Kate were quite disheartened, but also didn't want Aaron taking a risk he wasn't comfortable with. We then brought in an investment banker colleague of mine to help sell the company and he did just that. Aaron was retained by the new owner, who gave him a small equity stake in the company, and he is doing well with the new owners. Jerry and Kate are traveling around the country visiting their children and grandchildren and playing golf whenever they can.

It's important to know there's quite a difference in service offering between a business broker and an investment banker. Typically, brokers list companies for sale with a price, like a realtor lists a house. They may have expertise in analyzing or recasting financials or they may have come from an accounting or entrepreneurial background. Whatever their expertise, it usually aligns well with what smaller businesses need for representation. They tend to sell smaller, Main Street-type companies, usually under $5 million in revenue, but can sometimes go higher. Investment bankers have targets much higher. Some will work with smaller companies, but most do not, because the amount of work and expense involved in the process won't allow for it. They use data rooms and pitch books for generating interest in a company and they never quote a price, but rather seek to spur interest from as many parties as possible, like an auction where items go to the highest bidder. Sometimes private equity firms will put their hat in the ring and look for strategic acquisitions, giving the investment banker a larger pool of prospects. Check out the Business Value Assessment tool in the Appendix from Sunbelt Business Brokers, who provide services for both small and middle-market companies in need of investment banking services.

Ray and his dad Reggie co-owned a business that manufactured health and wellness products, selling them over a period of twenty-eight years to consumers, resellers, and medical professionals. In their quest for planning the perfect exit for Reggie, they learned that their business was worth far less than they needed for Reggie to retire. To compound the problem, Reggie was ill and needed to step aside from leading the company. When I met with Ray, I learned that Reggie had been using a great deal of the company's cash for his personal use, jeopardizing their ability to cover expenses when sales were flat. The fastest way for them to grow and support Reggie's retirement was to acquire other companies, but they lacked the cash to do it. Once we turned their financial house around, we were in a better position to acquire. We brought in an investment banker to help us find a company we could afford with the right product mix and culture. Since the acquisition was made, the integration of the two companies has been nearly seamless, which is highly unusual. However, with the right advisers in place and a clear picture of what you're looking for, acquiring another business can help you get to your exit destination faster than growing your business organically.

As long as a match in culture is at the top of your criteria list, you'll have a good shot at a successful integration.

Reggie and Ray's company sales have quadrupled since the acquisition and their future growth potential is brighter than ever.

CHAPTER 5 **CHECKLIST**

☐ Consider the pros and cons of selling internally or externally.

☐ If you're focused on internal sale, begin thinking about a plan to groom your successor.

☐ If external seems your path, begin to research your options and seek competent advice. See the resource in the Appendix from Sunbelt Business Advisers on page 110.

☐ Meet with a few brokers or investment bankers to get a feel for their role and services.

☐ Put together a timeline for exit (not carved in stone, just a target).

☐ Meet with other stakeholders—if you haven't already—to get feedback and share your initial plan.

☐ If you haven't met with your business attorney in a while, now would be a good time to start getting your legal house in order. See the checklist on page 106 from Best and Flanagan.

CHAPTER 5
QUOTES BY FAMOUS WOMEN

"Trying to do it all and expecting that it all can be done exactly right is a recipe for disappointment. Perfection is the enemy."

—SHERYL SANDBERG, COO OF FACEBOOK

STATISTIC

"Nearly 50 percent of all privately held businesses will suffer from at least one of the five D's in their business life cycle." (Exit Planning Institute)

Exit Planning Institute. "2017 State of Business Owner Readiness Survey Twin Cities Metro Area". *Exit Planning Institute*, 2017. https://exit-planning-institute.org/

Chapter 6

Where Do You Want To Go?

Life would be so much more fun and less stressful if we had a better handle on timing; but since we can't predict the future, at least not until there's an app for that, we're left with doing our best to apply what we know to be true now and not to repeat the mistakes of the past.

In Lewis Carroll's *Alice in Wonderland*, Alice and the Cheshire Cat shared this exchange:

Alice asked the Cheshire Cat, who was sitting in a tree, "What road do I take?"

The cat replied, "Where do you want to go?"

"I don't know," Alice answered.

"Then," said the cat, "it really doesn't matter, does it?"

As business owners, we feel the most lost when we don't know our next move. Having a plan will help eliminate the lost feeling and bring about more feelings of having found that next move. A newfound sense of peace will be the fruit of your labor when you plan a thoughtful, complete transition from your business. Imagine a better night's sleep and a sense of freedom like you've probably never had. This book is about doing yourself a favor and putting a plan in place to achieve this sense of peace, in case you hadn't figured that out already. Once you have a solid plan in place—and yes, plans can and do change—you can then explore what kind of timing you seek. How will you know your exit timeline if you don't know the value of your company or how you stand in the future of your financial plan? The more control you have over these foundational pieces, the more time you'll have to decide on the best options for you and your stakeholders. We're talking about good timing here versus poor timing. Few things in life could be worse than being backed into a corner with no options after you've spent your entire life building your business.

Of course, life can happen and catch us off-guard. (Remember the five Ds? I had three occur in my life simultaneously.) If you and your company are prepared and ready to make a transition, you'll weather an unplanned storm a lot easier and with less fall-out than if you're caught without a net. When you have a good plan, you can be nimble, make better decisions and not risk high losses.

Jennifer was introduced to me by her fractional chief financial officer (CFO), Kyle. (A fractional CFO is a consultant who acts as a part time CFO for owners of smaller companies, helping them make financial decisions by weighing scenarios, creating financial budgets, and generating forecasts and plans for growth.) Kyle and I had breakfast one morning and he confided in me that he had taken the company as far as he could and needed someone with some soft skills to come in and direct Jennifer and her mother, Jane. Jane had started the company thirty years prior and had been successful in formulating healthcare products for consumer use. Being more of a scientist than a business-builder, Jane managed to grow her lifestyle while the company grew, depleting its profits by drawing large distributions and using the business to pay for her personal expenses. No matter what Kyle's advice was about not using the business as an ATM and keeping a good amount of cash in the company, Jane refused to listen. Kyle shared that Jane's current health issues with Multiple Sclerosis kept her from being able to continue leading the company as she had been, and Jennifer was now in charge.

Jennifer had been an employee of the business for about ten years at that point. Everyone loved her gentle, professional approach to management. She respected each of her employees and they returned that respect with loyalty and hard work. Jane's relationship with the staff was also strong, and they enjoyed being given the autonomy to handle their roles without micro-management from either of the owners. The staff members were also empathetic toward their fearless leader, Jane, and her debilitating health issues, especially since none of the company's patented formulations were designed to help with MS. Jane's MS onset came without warning and shocked everyone, since she had always been the epitome of wellness for a woman her age.

Kyle confided in me, "Julie, Jane doesn't have an exit strategy and she won't listen to me. I've been an adviser to the company for five years now, so my voice doesn't seem to have the impact it used to have. I think we need someone fresh to work with her and Jennifer to get this succession plan in place before something worse happens to Jane."

"I'd be happy to meet with them, Kyle," I replied. "Let's see what we can do to help them eliminate some risk and increase their legacy odds. Chances are that Jane's symptoms will lessen if we can reduce the stress she's under."

Jane and I met and talked about her wishes for leaving a legacy and how long she'd like to stay on. She knew her health would get in the way of remaining long term, but at age sixty-four she still felt she had a few good years left. She admitted to me that she had not managed the business side of her company well and to top it off, she didn't have a good financial plan in place to secure her lifestyle after retirement. Her numerous spending sprees were costing her a lot more than she'd realized. She said sadly, "Julie, I wish I had met you ten or fifteen years ago. You could have set me straight then and I wouldn't be in such a timing conundrum now." Unfortunately, that expression is one I've heard over and over from my clients: "If only we'd met sooner."

Why do you think we as business owners hesitate when we have an opportunity to hire an adviser who can help us get through the exit process? I think one issue is, as humans, we tend to resist change, even if the change could be positive. Until the pain of staying the same is greater than the perceived pain of change, the change will not come. It's all about timing. In my travels, I've met with hundreds of business owners and only about 25 percent of them have become my clients. Why? Aside from the fact that I'm not the best at selling, I think it's about timing. When I meet with a potential client, it has to coincide with when they feel ready, which is where a crystal ball would come in handy. With the advisers I've hired over the years, I, too, wondered about whether I'd get my money's worth. The fees are a bit to get over, but once you get a rhythm down, the fees are moot. As I work with owners, I become a part of their team. Frankly, there's no way you could hire someone on staff who does all that I do for as little as I charge. I tell my clients I'm the lowest cost, biggest return non-employee they'll ever have.

After about a year of working with Jennifer on growing revenue and decreasing costs in the business, I sat down again with Jane to share my advice for going forward.

"Jane," I began, "Jennifer and I have done all we can with what we have to improve the company's bottom line. At this point I will say that we're going to need to make more big changes to the Profit & Loss Statement and your Balance Sheet in order for us to build enterprise value and for you to be able to retire. We should decrease your compensation again and completely stop having the company pay your personal expenses. There's no way this company can support your lifestyle as it is into the future and remain a going concern. You don't have to leave the business entirely unless you want to, but your compensation is still out of normal range and it's preventing Jennifer from being able to implement the growth strategies we've been working on. We simply need the capital to do what we need to do."

It wasn't an easy conversation to have, but Jane replied, "Okay, but how do I build my retirement accounts if my compensation is reduced again? You know I'm not financially prepared to retire."

I said, "Let's meet with your financial adviser and see what creative ideas he has to help us figure this out. Knowing Ryan, he'll have a few options up his sleeve."

Another year passed, and Jane's health continued to deteriorate, but slower than her doctors predicted. She was able to stay on as a liaison to their strategic partners and as a mentor to the company's lab technicians. Through her newfound frugality, her savings were considerably increased. Even though she had to work longer than she had anticipated, she saw light at the end of the tunnel. She also completed her estate plan, naming Jennifer as sole shareowner upon her death. Jane was a single person, and being that Jennifer was her only child, their succession plan wasn't as complicated as some. Jane realized she was holding her own daughter back from success and made swift changes and improvements to rectify this problem.

Fast-forward to a year ago, when Jennifer retained the services of an investment banker to search for a strategic acquisition of another company. It was the perfect timing to acquire, as their market was consolidating, and older owners were looking for a way out. Both Jane and Jennifer have changed the outcome for themselves and the future legacy of their business. You can too, even if you own a smaller company like Jane and Jennifer did.

CHAPTER 6 **CHECKLIST**

☐ What does "leaving a legacy" mean to you?

☐ If you haven't already, list your advisers
in order of best to least on how well they
know your business and how much you trust
their advice.

☐ If you've never hired a consultant to help
you, now would be a good time. Exit
planning is not DIY and your other advisers
don't have the bandwidth or expertise to
coordinate the process.

☐ Begin to picture a 'best case' scenario for
your exit. Who's involved, how would you like
it to occur, when would you like to be fully
transitioned out? What will your life be like
afterwards?

☐ Preparing you and your business for a
sale could cost 10 to 20 percent of the
sale price, depending on whether you sell
internally or externally, especially if you're
having to get yourself and your business
caught up in preparation. That's why now is
the time to start, so you can avoid all that
expense all at once.

CHAPTER 6
QUOTES BY FAMOUS WOMEN

"I kind of define power now by having the confidence to make your own decisions, to not be swayed by other people, and be brave and fearless to know that, even if you do make the wrong decision, you made it for a good reason."

—ADELE

"A man told me that for a woman, I was very opinionated. I said for a man you're kind of ignorant."

—ANNE HATHAWAY

STATISTIC

"13 percent of women owned companies have been in business twenty years or more." (SCORE)

Annie Pilon, "20 Amazing Stats on Women Entrepreneurs from SCORE," Smallbiztrends (website), accessed January 24, 2020, https://smallbiztrends.com/2018/06/women-entrepreneurs-statistics.html

©Glasbergen
glasbergen.com

"Are you concerned about age discrimination? I noticed you printed your resume on Sponge Bob stationery."

Chapter 7

Your Life 2.0: What Could That Look Like?

I hate to be Captain Obvious here, but women are different than men. I know you've already read about and heard all the ways we're not the same but let me add one more. When it comes to business exit, women and men approach it differently.

As a woman and a business owner, you've worn many hats. You've been entrepreneur, bread winner, homemaker, mom, and wife, all at the same time. Usually when the time comes for you to consider selling your business, the kids are grown and gone or close to it, or you've reached a milestone birthday, or both, and you're wondering, "What else is there?" If that's the case, I can empathize. I swam in those shark-infested waters for many years. My hope is that through the questions at the end of this chapter, you will be able to take a few steps closer to imagining what your life could look like after business. I hope, too, that you can think big and not deny yourself the dreams you may have put on hold for so long that you've forgotten about them.

For those of you who can't imagine what life after your business would be like, and you feel a sense of loss or fear, I get it, but please stay with me. For those of you who have it all mapped out and you can't wait to turn over the keys to your empire, I applaud your courage to look ahead at what could be. Either way, your newfound freedom is right around the corner. And whether you've planned out your future life or not, I'd encourage you to ponder the checklist, because chances are pretty good you missed a thing or two. I can honestly say that as I do my life's work, all the ownership and business experiences I've had set me up to be able to deliver the services my clients and audiences need and want. I see the work I do as sort of a social enterprise, because it really is life-changing.

If you're like most women business owners, you've had to do it all for so long that you may have lost touch with who you truly are as a person, aside from all that you do for others. If you've been a human doing versus a human being, you may be having a hard time returning to your former dreams. Do you wonder what it's like just to be? What would it take to turn off your thoughts and enjoy the beauty of your own backyard? The answers you seek are inside of you. What would it take for you to identify with your own longings? Insights will come when you listen and let your heart speak.

My experience consulting with men planning their exit brings about a similar issue when it comes to planning a next act, but in a different way, because men seem to make more time for leisure and fun in their life than women. When asked what they plan to do with their life after business, men usually rattle off a list of fun, leisurely activities that they already enjoy doing, such as golfing, fishing, hunting, and remodeling jobs. When I ask a woman the same question, however, I may get a shrug instead of an answer. When I do get an answer, a woman sees herself making a difference by volunteering or sitting on non-profit boards, but not much having to do with her own desires for fun and adventure. Not that fun and adventure are the be-all and end-all when it comes to next act planning, but I would bet you've got some catching-up to do in that department.

Another area where men and women differ is that the fear of loss tends to be stronger in men than women. Men's sense of self and relevancy are tightly woven into their work. Think of when a man is out of work and how much more devasting it is to them than it is for women. A man's biggest concern is, "How will I remain relevant and productive without my business?" and "Who am I without my work?" Women do worry about those things too, but not as much for themselves as they do for their teams. They will ask, "What will happen with my employees if I sell?" and "How will anyone take care of this company the way *I* have?" Men can and do have the same concerns, but these concerns seem to be a bigger deal for women.

Knowing that there are similarities and differences between men and women in a business exit situation is all well and good, but it still boils down to getting to know yourself, which is more challenging today than ever. With the constant noise of ping and buzz from our Fitbit, cell phones, laptops, and all the other technology we live with, it's a wonder we can get any original thinking done. Creativity needs an outlet and some silence. You'll learn a lot about who *you* are, what you want, and when by listening to yourself and searching your heart. After all you've been through and the sacrifices you've made to build your business, you deserve to have your heart's desire. Let me encourage you to venture into the unknown of you so you can figure out what that is. And please try to have fun with it! This transition is not another chore, it's an adventure.

The story I know best on this subject happens to be my own, so let me share part of my quest to find a meaningful next act with you. Finding my way was quite a journey and I had to get comfortable with being uncomfortable. There were many wrong turns, bumps in the road, and detours, because going from mess to success takes time. As I shared in Chapter Two, for two decades I owned three businesses in the Twin Cities area with my former husband. Working together, owning three companies, and raising four children took a heavy toll on our marriage and over time we drifted apart. When I went through the simultaneous life changes of divorce, selling the businesses, and splitting our assets and our family life, I had a hard time finding myself for a while. It was the emptiest time in my life. I still had my children, but only half of the time. My house, companies, and marriage were all gone. What would fulfill me I didn't know, but my journey to find out was one of self-discovery.

I started to enjoy the journey after I went through a dark, scary tunnel. During that time, I'd wonder, "Wasn't life supposed to be grand once I took the leap to make these long overdue changes?" I found the answer to be "yes," but only after the space between these changes was over. This period sits between an ending and a new beginning and it can't be rushed. It was then that I finally found a couple of great mentors and advisers to help me make it through. "If only I'd known these people years ago," I'd think to myself. But I hadn't. They came along when they were supposed to. Had they come earlier, I wouldn't have been ready for them. Just like this book: if the message doesn't resonate, you may not be ready for it. If that's the case, then put the book down and pick it up again in a year or two. You must be ready for the message in order to take the action necessary to get what you want.

Once I accepted that I was in the right place at the right time, I was able to indulge in some soul-searching. What was I passionate about? What was I good at? I knew I wanted to start another business, but I didn't know what it would be. To accelerate my decision making, I chose to approach my closest friends and family. "Surely they will help me know what to do," I thought.

It started with a questionnaire I found online that focused on life-coaching techniques. I put a list of ten questions together and sent them to my top ten besties, asking them to comment on my strengths and weaknesses. The questions were more general in nature but helped me know what they thought of me. I was happy and surprised to see so much consistency in their answers. This exercise brought me to the next, which was to pursue a handful of career options to see where I might fit in. The one that kept coming back was the opportunity to become a business coach. Three times I was approached over a period of six months to become one by different people. After the third inquiry, I decided to listen. So, I approached my top list and asked what they thought about me becoming a business coach. Every one of them had the same answer: a resounding, "Yes, that is exactly what you should do." This experience was edifying. A few years later, I added the Exit Planning credential to my business consulting practice and haven't looked back. Business consulting truly is my life's work. I didn't retire, but I moved on to doing something that brings me great joy and satisfaction. You can, too. You don't have to quit working, but how nice would it be if you only work because you want to, on your own terms, not because you must? That's what we're after here: options.

How can you use your gifts and talents to further your next act? Maybe you'll spend time at home and tend a larger garden, consult, volunteer at your place of worship, participate on boards or nonprofits, babysit your grandchildren, travel with your spouse or a friend, play more golf, teach yoga, hike the Grand Tetons, or learn how to play piano. Whatever it is, write down what resonates with you. Dream big, then read your dreams out loud and smile at yourself in the mirror when you're done. You're on the way.

CHAPTER 7 **CHECKLIST**

Where do I see myself in five years?

☐ What are my core values and how can I live them out in this next phase of life?

☐ What can I do to ensure my vision has a chance to succeed?

☐ What are some of the obstacles I may encounter, both personally and professionally?

☐ What parts of my previous work experience do I want to maintain or carry into another endeavor?

☐ How do I see my relationships changing after I retire and what can I do to prepare for these changes?

CHAPTER 7
QUOTES BY FAMOUS WOMEN

*"If you get, give.
If you learn, teach."*

—MAYA ANGELOU

❋

*"Your value will not be
what you know; it will be
what you share."*

—GINNI ROMETTY, CEO OF IBM

STATISTIC

"1.7 percent of all women owned firms have revenues of $1 million or more." (The 2018 State of Women Owned Businesses Report)

Ventureneer with the support of CoreWoman, commissioned by American Express, The 2018 State of Women-Owned Businesses Report, n.d., https://about.americanexpress.com/files/doc_library/file/2018-state-of-women-owned-businesses-report.pdf

"I bought out three lemonade stands this morning and made a 50% return on my investment by 4 o'clock. How was *your* day?"

Chapter 8

How Does Fear Stop You?

I saw a funny picture posted online of a woman getting a tattoo on her upper arm. It said, "No Regerts"—a permanent error by the artist that the patron would certainly regret! I want to warn you about looking back on the what if's and watch out for the temptation to doubt your decisions. As long as you have vetted your options well and have good advisers to guide you, then don't worry about making any permanent mistakes like the tattoo lady.

Yet it's common for us women to doubt ourselves; expect that you'll be tempted. We can doubt our decision to hire, fire, lay off, expand, launch, ship, spend, or save. We can also second-guess our decisions to exit our businesses.

As a business consultant and exit planner I've worked with a lot of women entrepreneurs. Some were sole owners, while others had partners. One thing that I have found in common among female entrepreneurs is that they can tend to second-guess the decisions that they make, especially the bigger decisions that have a heavier impact on the future. The decision of when and how to exit your business will probably be no exception to that pattern.

You may find yourself asking, "What if I would have hung on a little longer?" or speculating, "Maybe I could have gotten more money for the company." Decide ahead of time what you will say to yourself when you start feeling seller's remorse, because you probably will to some degree. Another common worry among women owners is "What will happen to my employees?" or "What if the owner makes changes that hurt the business?"

Are you afraid to make the move because you're afraid it will be the wrong one? Are you afraid of living a life that you would deem as less productive than the one you have now? What if you could be even more productive after business?

There is only one you. You have a song to sing that no one else can sing. I know you've heard all this before, but I think it's a good thing for us to remind each other about how unique and special we are. The gifts we have will continue to inspire and help other people as long as we use them; this is where personal fulfillment and joy reside.

I think the best part of life is the part where you get to make more fun and personal choices than you had in the past regarding how you use your time, whom you help, how you spend your money, and where you find yourself making a difference. I know that that has been the case for me.

Moving through the years in the business world as both employee and owner, I used to feel I had something I could contribute to help mankind in a big way and I was always focused on the big picture of what was possible. As I got older, I stopped trying to figure out how I could save the world and started focusing on making an impact one client at a time, one speech at a time, one book at a time.

Let's give credit where it's due; you've already made a huge impact on many lives. Have you ever written out all of the accomplishments of your life on one page? Putting yourself through school, acquiring credentials, getting married, birthing babies, raising kids, buying real estate, launching and running companies, winning awards. You've surely got quite the list. Consider the impact you've made on your family, friends, colleagues, customers, vendors, neighbors, and community. That's a big wow, girl.

You have the unique ability to do amazing things with your life, because you are living in an age where there are almost no limits to what you can accomplish. Imagine living in the 1920s; would you have had the same opportunities? Even in 1950 or

1960, opportunities for women were not even close to the opportunities available today. The sky really is the limit.

If you ever find that you have regrets of the past, I'd invite you to flip that bad memory over on its back and look at all the good that came from it. How was the struggle or poor decision a learning lesson that forced you to grow and helped get you where you are today? Fruit was definitely produced, you just may have to dig a little to find it.

Your future and your life are extremely bright, and I hope and pray that you will reach out to me and share what's going on in your life after business.

Let's not get all caught up in finding a purpose for your life. Our society seems rather bent on people finding a purpose like it's a new thing we have yet to discover. I'm going to bet you already know what you want to do next with your life. You at least know what you like to do and what's important to you. The reason I say this is because I think that we can over-analyze and over-think what it is we need and want. Perhaps we're asking ourselves, "Is this idea or plan big enough or important enough?" Given the fact that you've owned and built a successful business, I'm going out on a limb and saying whatever you do next will surely be big and important enough for you, whether you're planning to scale the Himalayas or scale another company, you're wired to make an impact. Whatever you want to do, just know you're *enough.*

If you're looking for a place to start, examine the communities that you are involved in currently. As you examine them, I want you to ask yourself, are they primarily business-related connections or personal connections? Are there causes I believe in? Will these relationships continue after I've made my transition? Is there an opportunity within this community or organization that I could become more involved? Would I consider these people to be my tribe or could they be? The checklist after this chapter will take you a bit deeper here.

Here's a story that illustrates one example of living out your next act. I had a client named Patty, who owned a counseling clinic for many years. She had several therapists working for her and she decided she didn't want to manage people anymore. She was making a good living, but she was tired of all the headaches from managing the staff and the operations. Though she did love being a therapist, she didn't love the ownership part of it, so she sold her clinic to an internal successor. Since she loved being a therapist and didn't agree to a noncompete agreement, she kept her most of her clients and started working independently.

Patty and I met through a mutual connection. During our first meeting, Patty shared, "I love my work, but

I need to make it more fun and therapeutic for my clients. I'd like some help from you, Julie, in creating a business plan and in helping me implement it. If I get stuck, I'm the kind of person that can stay stuck for a while."

"You've got a great vision for this, Patty," I replied. "Let's talk about how you could provide therapy services different than the norm."

Patty thought for a minute and said, "I think I'd like to get them outside!"

Fast forward six months, and a new method of providing therapy was born: walking side by side in the outdoors. In case of bad weather, they meet at nearby mall. Patty is meeting her clients within a twenty-mile radius of her office. They walk while they talk during their sessions. She came up with her therapy idea of meeting people at local parks, so she could do work she loves and combine it with another love: the outdoors.

Her clients love their sessions and she's doing well with her practice; it's just Patty and a contracted book-keeper. She travels a lot with her family and spends a lot more time at their second home on Lake Superior. She's happy, fulfilled, and still making a difference.

I read a book when my kids were teens about how powerful walking shoulder-to-shoulder with your kids can be. Children can have a hard time with eye-to-eye communication. Walking side-by-side takes away that intimidation they might feel and gives them a sense of togetherness, which helps open the door for honest dialogue. Patty realized this method could be a way for her to provide great therapy for her clients in a unique and healthy way.

In closing this book, I'm going to ask you to do some soul-searching and some research. The soul-searching is on your own. Try some journaling and reading some good nonfiction on subjects that help you think through what you could do or be in your next act. Find some life-transition books or personal development books and biographies of leaders you admire. One of the best I've read recently is by Seth Godin called *What to do When it's Your Turn*.

Try doing a personal SWOT Analysis, identifying your internal strengths and weaknesses, and external opportunities and threats to making your plan. This can be a great exercise in self-discovery if you're honest with yourself. Now, we women can tend to focus on our weaknesses, but I would encourage you not to do that. I challenge you to have twice as many strengths as weaknesses on your list.

The research part is in talking with your closest friends and family and asking them to help you explore what you could consider for your next act. If you are feeling unsure, you will find this especially helpful. I have to say it is fun to hear similar or even identical words from different people as they describe who they see you to be and what they think you're good at.

When my mother told me she thought I would make a great business adviser, that was wonderful to hear. Don't moms always say nice things? Well, she was not only being nice, she was being genuinely honest. It's okay to ask your parents their opinions (if you are blessed to still have them around). Try to also talk with people who are not in your family, who had not been lifelong friends, who had known you in only one aspect of your life. Perhaps you had a professional relationship with them, participated in a volunteer group with them, or knew them as a long-time neighbor. Don't necessarily ask people who you hang out with all the time or who know everything about you, but make sure they know enough to give you an honest opinion of how they view you. If you find yourself in a situation where you're not quite sure what your next move will be, but you know you want to do something, then this could be a great way for you to expand your horizons as you discover the wealth of talent you possess through the eyes of those who care about you and your happiness.

CHAPTER 8 **CHECKLIST**

☐ Make a list of non-negotiables or must-haves in your next act.

☐ Make a list of your top ten besties.

☐ Create a short questionnaire that your besties can answer to help in your discernment process for what's next in your life.

☐ Take a two-week vacation or staycation and spend as much time alone as possible.

☐ Meet with a trusted clergy member, mentor, or counselor to help you think through the coming chapter in your life.

"Would the woman with the thesaurus please sit down and be quiet?"

CHAPTER 8
QUOTES BY FAMOUS WOMEN

"I alone cannot change the world, but I can cast a stone across the waters to create many ripples."

—St. Mother Teresa

"Aerodynamically, the bumblebee shouldn't be able to fly, but the bumblebee doesn't know that so it goes on flying anyway."

—Mary Kay Ash

"Always be a first-rate version of yourself instead of a second-rate version of somebody else."

—Judy Garland

STATISTIC

"73 percent of small business owners do not have a team of professional advisers." (Exit Planning Institute)

Exit Planning Institute. "2017 State of Business Owner Readiness Survey". *Exit Planning Institute,* 2017. https://exit-planning-institute.org/

"Women-owned businesses employ over 8.4 million workers and generate $264 billion in payroll."

Michael J. McManus, "Get the Facts on Women Business Owners," *U.S. Department of Labor Blog,* July 5, 2017, https://blog.dol.gov/2017/07/05/get-facts-women-business-owners

Dore, Jason. "Despite Smaller Size, Women-Owned Businesses Have a Significant Economic Impact: The U.S. Small Business Administration." Small Business Administration, 31 May 2017, www.sba.gov/advocacy/despite-smaller-size-women-owned-businesses-have-significant-economic-impact.

The Tools and Checklists in the Appendix, along with several other free downloads can be found at poisedforexit.com.

Transition Planning Checklist

NAME

PHONE

WEBSITE

YRS IN BUSINESS

COMPANY

EMAIL

TYPE OF BUSINESS

OF EMPLOYEES

GROSS ANNUAL REVENUE

TEAM OF ADVISERS

Have you assembled a team of advisers, with whom you can discuss your transition options?

Please identify below all advisers you already have in place:

☐ Business/ M & A Attorney

   Name_____

☐ Estate Planning Attorney

   Name_____

☐ Certified Public Accountant (CPA)

   Name_____

☐ Wealth Manager

   Name_____

☐ Exit Planner

   Name_____

☐ Business Consultant or Coach

   Name_____

☐ Banker

   Name_____

☐ Other

   Name_____

Is each educated and practised in Transition and Succession planning? _____ Yes _____ No

Does the team meet quarterly on a specific Transition agenda, to ensure all perspectives and expertise are shared and all bases covered?

_____ Yes _____ No

STRATEGIC PLAN

Do you have a Strategic Plan? _____ Yes _____ No

☐ If you don't yet have one, create a Strategic Plan with the help of a business consultant/ coach who understands Exit Strategy well.

☐ Implement new strategies for growth and improvement to the business.

FINANCIALS

☐ Create as much 'curb appeal' as possible, but also ensure that your internal processes and documentation are accurate and in order, namely your financials. "True" them up now with the help of a good CFO. The look-back period from a potential buyer is typically 3 years.

☐ Don't use your business as an ATM.

☐ Discuss with your wealth manager whether to diversify your equity before the sale.

☐ Make sure your business is the proper tax entity well before the liquidity event.

☐ Have preliminary conversations with your CPA and Tax lawyer regarding how to save on taxes after the sale

EMPLOYEES & CULTURE

☐ Discuss key person employee retention programs with your wealth manager and M & A attorney.

☐ Implement these plans. The value of your key people to a potential buyer is higher than you think. You can't afford to lose them.

☐ Focus on growing the culture of your business and increasing employee engagement.

☐ Implement best practices in HR (recognition, compensation, onboarding, and regular reviews.)

BRAND & IP

☐ Update and document all internal processes, trade secrets and other Intellectual Property

☐ Utilize the services of an IP attorney to register or update trademarks, patents and copyrights

☐ Focus on brand development with the help of a brand/ marketing expert

☐ Promote the brand; it should be one of your most important assets and goes far beyond your "reputation" in the marketplace.

MARKETING

☐ Update your marketing plan.

☐ Revise your website with your newly-refreshed brand and brand messaging.

☐ Implement a digital marketing plan with measurable ROI.

☐ Blog.

☐ Raise your "Net Promoter Score."

NEXT ACT PLANNING

Start working on a plan for your Next Act. You still have a lot of life to live, so plan it out so you can maintain your sense of relevance and productivity.

Answer these questions:

☐ Do you have enough to retire?

_____ Yes _____ No

☐ Do you WANT to retire?

_____ Yes _____ No

☐ Is there another business in your future?

_____ Yes _____ No

☐ How will you spend your time after you retire?

SUCCESSORSHIP

If you DO have an Internal Successor:

☐ Begin with hiring a consultant to do assessments measuring leadership and business acumen.

☐ Have candid conversations about goals, desires and expectation.

☐ Be very clear on what your new role will be; ensure that everyone in the company knows it.

☐ Make sure that terms of financing the deal are planned and agreed upon far in advance with agreements in writing.

☐ Visit with your banker well ahead of time, so that you understand what's allowed and not allowed in financing a deal.

☐ Obtain recommendations and meet with 2 or 3 Investment Bankers or Business Brokers (which one will depend on the size of your business.)

☐ Establish a relationship now, so they know you and your business well when the time comes to put it on the market.

☐ Meet with your business attorney at least annually to update him or her on your plans. Determine whether there are there any steps needed to de-risk the business from a legal standpoint well in advance.

To download, go to PoisedforExit.com/tools-for-download

Financial Planning Starter Questions

1. In your mind, how long do you think it will take to financially prepare so you can support your lifestyle and exit someday from your business?

2. Do you know the current Enterprise Value of your business?

3. When you think about a 'bucket list', what are some of the things that you've always wanted to do?

   • Do you know whether you can afford to do these things without a paycheck?

4. What are your Legacy goals? *Do you have philanthropic aspirations? *Do you want your business to be carried into the next generation? *Do you want to invest in other businesses? *Do you have any Trusts in place and if so, are you familiar with their type and purpose?

5. Do you have a Buy Sell or Shareholder Agreement?

   • Is it current?

   • Is it funded?

6. Is it time to update your Estate Plan? Refer to the resource from Dunlap Seeger on page 105.

   • Have you done any tax planning in advance to prepare for your future liquidity event?

7. Do you have Contingency Planning in place in the event of your untimely absence from the business? *Are your heirs and leadership team prepared for what to do in case something happens?

8. How much and what types of insurance do you have to

protect you and your family in the event one of the 5 Ds occurs? Consider having an audit done of all your insurance policies.

9. How will you replace the paycheck you are currently receiving from the business?

To download, go to PoisedforExit.com/tools-for-download

Accounting Checklist

1. Are your financials in compliance with US GAAP? Have they been audited or reviewed three years?

2. Do you have significant customer concentrations or significant customer contracts coming up for renewal? How would a transaction effect those customer relationships?

3. Has the company changed any significant accounting policies in the last three years? If yes, do you understand what impact these changes may have on company value?

4. Do you know the effects of recent accounting standards changes (ex. Revenue recognition; lease accounting; etc)?

5. Do you know what the key value drivers of your business are (e.g. fixed or intangible assets, customer base) and how they will be successfully transferred through a transaction?

6. Do you have a sense as to how much your business is worth?

7. Do you have well thought out, up-to-date budgets and financial projections?

8. Have you identified and summarized one-time or non-recurring expense or revenue items to understand adjusted EBITDA?

9. Are the financial statements prepared consistently on a monthly basis? Are there quarterly or year-end adjustments that should be accounted for monthly?

10. Do you know the sufficient level of working capital the business requires to fund on-going operations?

11. Would there be a significant capital investment for a buyer to operate the business?

12. Do you know what your monthly cash flow is? Is this something that is tracked and reviewed by management?

13. Do you understand the profitability with your customers, revenue lines, product mix etc.?

14. What does your customer churn rate look like?

15. Are your internal processes and controls appropriate to the size of the company? Are they documented?

To download, go to PoisedforExit.com/tools-for-download

Basic Estate Planning Checklist For Business Owners

Basic Documents Needed

☐ Powers of Attorney

☐ Health Care Directives

☐ Wills or Revocable Living Trusts

Other Common Components

☐ Irrevocable Trusts for Estate Tax Planning (SLATs, Dynasty Trusts, GRATs, Etc.)

☐ Family Limited Partnerships

☐ Life Insurance Planning (Consider ILITs)

☐ Charitable bequest planning

Key Considerations

Distribution Plan:
- Equal v. Equitable Distribution of Assets
- Vesting ages for beneficiaries

Overlapping Business Issues:
- Buy/sell agreements (funding with life insurance?)
- Valuations
- Liabilities - personal guaranties?
- Plan for owned real estate

Estate Tax Planning (both Federal and State):
- Gift Planning
- Maximizing use of spousal exemptions

Probate Avoidance:
- Consider Using Trusts and Transfer on Death Deeds
- Coordinate Titling and Beneficiary Designations

Fiduciary Selection:
- Trustees, Personal Representative/Executor
- Family/Friends v. Institutional

DUNLAP
SEEGER

David M. Pederson
Phone: 507-288-9111   Email: dmp@dunlaplaw.com

When it's Time to Explore "What's Next?"

BEST & FLANAGAN

Initial Legal Considerations When Planning a Sale or Other Transition of Your Business

You've built a business that you're proud of, but it's time to think about what comes next. Perhaps a competitor or outside investor has approached you with an enticing offer. Or a family member or key employee(s) has shown interest in leading your business into the future. Whatever the reason, you're thinking about "What's Next?" and how to move on to a new phase of your and/or your business's life.

Where do you start with assessing where your business currently stands and how it might influence your next adventure, whether that's a quiet retirement or making your favorite hobby your next business venture? The questions and topics below are intended to direct a business owner toward an inward-looking assessment of where their company currently stands and whether a plan needs to be implemented to better position the business for a sale or transfer, or if the business, if sold "as-is," will garner a transition that fits the owner's future plans.

The subjects and topics below cover many of the key categories that are explored during the "due diligence" phase of a potential business sale or transition. By reviewing, analyzing and assessing these topics internally and in collaboration with legal and other trusted advisors, business owners can begin to think about and plan for a transition while also considering what else might need to be done before it really is time to move forward.

This list is not intended to constitute legal advice or to create any form of attorney-client relationship.

1. If you were to sell your business tomorrow, in an ideal scenario, where would you be and what would you be doing the day after the sale? Do you retire? Do you continue to work?

2. What parts of operating your business give you drive, purpose and/or happiness? What causes you the most stress and/or anxiety?

3. How prepared are you for a "disaster scenario"? If a key owner were to die or become permanently disabled, are one or more fail safes in place to keep the company operating with little or no disruption? Who would assume that ownership and/or control?

4. What are your company's greatest strategic strengths? What have you done in the past 5 to 10 years to invest in and build on those strengths and to create others?

5. How has the COVID-19 pandemic affected your business? Have you made any operational or organizational changes to better address and adapt to the "new normal"?

6. What are the largest potential risks to your company? What steps have you taken to manage and minimize those risks?

7. What percentage of your company's total revenue is attributable to its 5 largest customers/clients?

8. Does your business face consistent competition? If so, how are you positioned in relation to your most significant competitors?

9. Is your company reliant on sales or other business activities that originate outside of the United States? Is your company facing any supply chain or logistics challenges?

10. How do handle your company's accounting needs? Do you employ a full time or part time/fractional CFO? Do you engage outside accountants to prepare periodic financial statements?

11. Does your company have any secured or unsecured debt? What is the status of your company's relationship with its primary bank and/or lender(s)?

12. How many people do you employ and is turnover an issue? Do you have benefit/incentive programs in place to bolster recruiting and retention?

13. How is your company managed? Do you have a board of directors and do they meet regularly? What is the status of your corporate/organizational documents, such as minute books, stock records, bylaws, operating agreements and buy/sell agreements?

14. Has your company been engaged in any litigation, regulatory compliance investigations or audits (OSHA, NLRB, state or local licensing, etc.) or other disputes or formal legal claims in the past 5 years? If so, have those matters been resolved or are any ongoing?

15. Does your company have any significant operating contracts, such as licenses, leases, supply agreements or long-term sales contracts? Are all such agreements in good standing? Do you know whether any are transferrable and pursuant to what terms?

16. Does your company hold any registered intellectual property, such as trademarks, copyrights or

patents? Is your business heavily reliant on a particular brand, logo, name or other similar unregistered intellectual property? Are you aware of any unauthorized use of your company's intellectual property?

Best & Flanagan's Business & Corporate Law team is ready to meet you where you are at, in any phase of your transition. For more information, please visit www.bestlaw.com.

To download, go to PoisedforExit.com/tools-for-download

Sunbelt Business Brokers Value Assessment

BUSINESS VALUE	Customers & Revenue	Industry & Competition	People & Processes	Products & Suppliers
HIGH	• No customer more than 5% of revenue • National customers • Full sales team wins & retains business • Recurring revenue model	• Large & rapidly growing market • Little government • Market leader	• Experienced Management team • Proven information systems & processes in place • People and processes can handle growth	• Service or Product is a "must have" • Significant amount of revenue driven by proprietary products • No supplier more than 10% of revenue and/or redundant suppliers • Exclusive supplier relationships
MEDIUM	• No customer more than 10% of revenue • Regional & Local customers • Dedicated sales people • Some recurring revenue	• Modest market growth • Some government intervention • Business tends to trend with the economy • Average market share	• Some management but ownership still heavily involved • Some information systems and processes but not integrated	• Product or Service is a "should have" • No supplier more than 20% of revenue or redundant suppliers • Favorable supplier relationships
LOW	• Large Customer Concentrations • Small local customers • Owner handles most customers • Large project based revenue	• Small market that is flat or shrinking • Cyclical business • Many competitors	• No management, owner-centric • No professional accounting • Limited information systems	• Product is discretionary • No intellectual property • Large supplier concentrations

SUNBELT.®

BUSINESS ADVISORS

© Chris Jones - Sunbelt Business Advisors

To download, go to PoisedforExit.com/tools-for-download

110

"As of 2017, more than 11.6 million firms are owned by women in the United States, which generate over $1.7 Trillion in annual sales." National Association of Women Business Owners

"Women Business Owner Statistics," National Association of Women Business Owners (website), accessed January 24, 2020, https://www.nawbo.org/resources/women-business-owner-statistics.

Ventureneer with the support of CoreWoman, commissioned by American Express, *The 2017 State of Women-Owned Businesses Report,* n.d., https://about.americanexpress.com/sites/americanexpress.newshq.businesswire.com/files/doc_library/file/2017_SWOB_Report_-FINAL.pdf

"Women owned firms account for 39% of all privately held firms." NAWBO

Ventureneer with the support of CoreWoman, commissioned by American Express, *The 2017 State of Women-Owned Businesses Report,* n.d., https://about.americanexpress.com/sites/americanexpress.newshq.businesswire.com/files/doc_library/file/2017_SWOB_Report_-FINAL.pdf

5.4 Million firms are majority-owned by women of color in United States (BizBuySell.com) Change to NAWBO

Ventureneer with the support of CoreWoman, commissioned by American Express, *The 2017 State of Women-Owned Businesses Report,* n.d., https://about.americanexpress.com/sites/americanexpress.newshq.businesswire.com/files/doc_library/file/2017_SWOB_Report_-FINAL.pdf

From 1997-2017, women owned businesses grew by 114% compared to the national growth rate of 44% for all businesses. (BizBuySell.com)

American Express, and CoreWoman. "Summary of Key Trends." *The 2017 State of Women Owned Businesses Report,* Commissioned by American Express, 2017, about.americanexpress.com/sites/americanexpress.newshq.businesswire.com/files/doc_library/file/2017_SWOB_Report_-FINAL.pdf.

"79% of small business owners have no written transition plan." Survey Data from the Exit Planning Institute

"Nearly 50% of all privately held businesses will suffer from at least one of the 5 D's in their business life cycle." Research done by the Exit Planning Institute

"13% of Women Owned Companies have been in business twenty years or more." SCORE

Pilon, Annie. "20 Amazing Stats on Women Entrepreneurs from SCORE." *Small Business Trends*, 18 June 2018, smallbiztrends.com/2018/06/women-entrepreneurs-statistics.html.

"1.7% of all women owned firms have revenues of $1 million or more."

American Express, and CoreWoman. "Summary of Key Trends." The 2018 State of Women Owned Businesses Report, Commissioned by American Express, 2018, https://about.americanexpress.com/files/doc_library/file/2018-state-of-women-owned-businesses-report.pdf

"73% of small business owners do not have a team of professional advisers." Exit Planning Institute, State of Owner Readiness Survey Twin Cities Metro Area, 2017

"Women-owned businesses employ over 8.4 million workers and generate $264 billion in payroll." Small Business Administration

Dore, Jason. "Despite Smaller Size, Women-Owned Businesses Have a Significant Economic Impact: The U.S. Small Business Administration." *Small Business Administration*, 31 May 2017, www.sba. gov/advocacy/despite-smaller-size-women-owned-businesses-have-significant-economic-impact.

Acknowledgments

First of all, I would be nowhere in my exit-planning career if it weren't for the many wonderful business owner clients over the years. They taught me so much about their industries and their distinctive views on entrepreneurism. They allowed me to walk alongside them through the process of growing and improving their companies. Many of those clients I also helped navigate the process of exit planning (even before I became a certified exit planner). Together we did our best to de-risk and prepare them and their companies for an eventual sale. For those I don't see often, my hope is they are living a life they love and checking things off their bucket list. To *all* of them, it was an honor being your adviser and watching you grow; thank you for that.

My editor and publisher Henry DeVries has been more than an editor and publisher to me. His generous sharing of industry knowledge and instructional expertise has been a huge benefit for me in writing this book. He encouraged me through my bouts with self-doubt and fostered the confidence I needed to write it in the first place. I wasn't sure if women entrepreneurs would be interested in reading a book about exit planning, but since there are so many women entrepreneurs in the United States (11+ million, actually) Henry assured me that *some* of them would be. Thank you, Henry, for putting up with my delays and revisions, and thank you for your commitment to the success of the women you represent at Indie Books. You made a tough process easier by having such a great sense of humor and an empathetic heart. I'll be forever grateful to you for that.

To my husband, Shaun, who read and reread draft after draft. Who took on most of my share of the household chores, so I could write (for months). Who waited patiently for me many times while I had to "write one more paragraph" before we could leave for an event or a bike ride. Thank you for giving me your honest feedback and for believing that I could write (and finish) this book. Even though it's not a long book, it was one of the many simultaneous business endeavors I managed, and you let me be the overachiever that I am without a word to hold me back. You really do have "the patience of Job." I love you, Honey!

To my parents, Henry and Nancy, who taught me that working for yourself and being successful is possible if you want it bad enough. I will always remember listening to Zig Ziglar tapes in the car with you when I was a teen. I often still recall his inspirational, motivational messages in my everyday life. Mom and Dad, through your example and direction, I grew in my faith in God, which to this day is an integral part of who I am and how I operate. From you I also learned persistence, optimism, goal-setting, and grit. You helped me to believe I could do it and so I did. Thank you for everything. I love you.

To my children—Tyler, Ryan, Natalie, and Heather—how lucky you make me feel to be your mom and how proud I am of you all. Thank you for your support and love; it keeps me going. To Amber, Shaun, Jessa and Alicia, my wonderful loving stepchildren. Thank you for letting me be your "bonus Mom." I love you all.

To the Exit Planning Institute and its owners, Chris and Scott Snider. Thank you for having the courage and foresight to take EPI into the stratosphere. Your fortitude and commitment to the exit-planning industry has been a major catalyst for expanding awareness and education among advisers from across professional disciplines, fostering collaboration and affecting the exit outcomes for thousands (maybe millions) of privately held businesses for years to come. You are to be commended for this vision and for your work, and I am so grateful to be a part of the EPI family of advisers.

Lastly, I would like to thank my many colleagues in the profession of exit planning. For all I've learned from you and for the friendships we have forged, I will be eternally grateful. I would especially like to thank and acknowledge Nicki Vincent, Executive Director for ACG MN, Best and Flanagan, Dunlap Seeger, and all the other firms and advisers who influenced me, collaborated with me, and otherwise supported this project. Your collective commitment to business owners achieving a successful exit is exemplary and I am honored to collaborate with you in bringing essential tools together for the benefit of my readers.

The Tools and Checklists from these contributors are available for free download at poisedforexit.com

Julie Keyes was born and raised in a small suburb of Minneapolis, Minnesota. She is the oldest of three girls. Both of her parents were self-employed and instilled in her a strong work ethic. She was taught from a young age that life is what you make it. Her grandparents on both sides were business owners as well; you could say entrepreneurism was in her blood.

After college, she spent the next twenty-seven years in the mortgage and title insurance industry; twenty-three of those years she owned and operated several companies with her former husband. During those twenty-three years, she had four children. Managing four companies in three locations and raising four kids made for some *very* busy times.

As an employer, her primary duty was to manage the operations and business development for the companies. Her husband, a lawyer, ran the technical side of the business. Running a small business requires wearing many hats; some of them not well. Juggling trade shows, baseball games, client meetings, and dance lessons were a part of everyday life for a long time with many tough lessons learned. The ups and downs of business ownership and trying to be a good wife and mother at the same time were taxing, thrilling, and rewarding.

In 2010, Julie got divorced, bought her own house, quit her job, and launched KeyeStrategies, a business consulting firm all within six months. She spent the next five years building the business, acquiring clients and helping them improve and grow their companies. In 2015, she became a Certified Exit Planning Adviser (CEPA) through the Exit Planning Institute (EPI) and has grown her firm and her reputation as a leader in the exit-planning industry, both locally and nationally, as a sought-after consultant, speaker, and instructor.

In 2016, Julie launched the Twin Cities Metro Area Chapter for EPI and has since co-organized several large-scale exit-planning educational events for business owners. She is also a faculty member for EPI and was 2017 Leader of the Year. Julie originally launched *Poised for Exit* just after the onset of the COVID-19 pandemic, which required a shift in plans, since nearly all her speaking engagements got cancelled due to the lockdowns. She quickly had to pivot, so she accelerated the launch of her podcast show *Poised for Exit* in order to provide virtual, timely content for business owners. Since the launch of the show in June of 2020, the book and the show have grown a very healthy list of fans and followers among advisers and owners alike. You can find the book and Kindle version on Amazon or Barnes and Noble, and the podcast can be found on all major podcast platforms or go to poisedforexit.com. Julie is also the creator and producer of several self-paced, online courses. For more information on these visit keyestrategies.com

Julie's passion for helping business owners exit on their own terms (not someone else's) shines through in her actions as a local and national leader in the field. As a woman entrepreneur and one who experienced her own business exit in 2009, she dedicates this book to all the women business owners who read it. A business transition for a woman has its own nuances and this book is meant to help women navigate those waters as early and successfully as possible, so they can move on with peace, poise, and anticipation of an exciting next act, whatever that may be.

Made in USA - Kendallville, IN
17902_9781957651026
01.10.2023 1422